A Woman's Spirit

T0057290

A Woman's Spirit

More Meditations for Women

KAREN CASEY

Hazelden
Publishing

Hazelden Publishing
Center City, Minnesota 55012
hazelden.org/bookstore

ISBN: 978-0-89486-869-6

Editor's note:
A Woman's Spirit was originally published by its author, Karen Casey, as
an anonymous work.

This publication is not intended as a substitute for the advice of health
care professionals.

In the process of being reissued in 2020, A Woman's Spirit has under-
gone minor editing updates and been retypeset in the Whitman font
family.

To the greatest degree possible, the accuracy of quotations and sources
has been verified.

Hazelden Publishing offers a variety of information on addiction and
related areas. Our publications do not necessarily represent Hazelden's
programs nor do they officially speak for any Twelve Step organization.

Alcoholics Anonymous, AA, and the Big Book are registered trade-
marks of Alcoholics Anonymous World Services, Inc.

24 23 22   2 3 4 5 6

Cover design: Terri Kinne
Typesetting: Jessica Ess, Hillspring Books
Developmental editor: Heather Silsbee
Production editor: Victoria Tirrel

Introduction

I am so happy to be meeting you once again through these pages. This journey you and I are on has been full of surprises. Who could have imagined all the joys that have come to us? We have suffered setbacks too, but knowing we have the support of one another has helped us survive. What lies ahead for any of us remains a mystery, but we do know now, even though we occasionally forget, that the God of our understanding travels with us.

We are incredibly lucky women. No other group of people has the steady assurance that our program gives us every moment of our lives. All we have to do is remember to use the tools we have been given, be willing to listen to and love one another, and quietly pray to our God for direction and comfort. Because we are human, not perfect, we often need reminders of "how it works." That's the intent of this book.

I am just like you. I have no special knowledge of what makes one's life meaningful. Simply, I have consistently done what the Big Book tells me to do. I go to meetings, generally three a week, including Al-Anon. I stay in touch daily with sponsors and friends. I keep no secrets, and I willingly make amends rather than go to bed in discomfort. What I have written here and in other books has simply come to me.

I believe we all have within us the wisdom and knowledge to pass through any experience in life. Because of our fears, we sometimes block the guidance that's trying to reach us. It is my hope that these meditations can help move you beyond your fears.

We need each other, you and me. None of us can make this journey alone—not with any real joy and sanity, at least. I know of no magic, but I do know that the promises outlined by the founders of Alcoholics Anonymous will be fulfilled if we follow their suggestions and invite one another to travel with us. This is my invitation to you. Come with me through the pages of this book. Help me in my recovery, and I will help you. I do believe that is God's most meaningful lesson. Together, with faith and perseverance, we can create the kind of tomorrow we long for today. Thank you for being here.

JANUARY

God does not require that we be successful, only that we be faithful.
　　　　　　　　　　　　　　　　—*Mother Teresa*

It's probable we have never equated success with faith. Being successful meant accomplishing worthy goals and receiving the expected praise. We may have even considered that relying on faith to help us was a cop-out. Fortunately, so much about how we interpret life has changed since joining this journey through recovery.

In Step Three we learn that God wants us to have faith. We are coming to see, in fact, that acting as if we have faith begins to feel like faith. Coming to believe that God's only expectation is that we turn within for guidance makes every circumstance far less threatening.

Practicing faith promises that we will begin to feel successful in all our experiences because we are walking through them peacefully, trusting fully that God is at hand. Believing in God, being truly faithful, can be the greatest success of our lives.

I can be faith filled today if I turn my life and my will over to the care of God. I will remind myself of this every time I get in the "driver's seat."

Watching a child acquire language, I realize, again,
that naming things demystifies them.

—Mary Casey

Sharing with another woman our fears of starting a new
job, ending a relationship, getting into therapy, or even
joining a social club will help us keep the fear in perspective. Fears that go undiscussed have a way of growing
and overtaking our lives. In time we find that because of
our shame about being afraid, we have isolated ourselves
from the very people who can help us.

All of us are afraid some of the time. Our fears, however, can be managed if we use the tools found in this
fellowship. Sponsors, friends, and meetings are the channels for our release from fear. Naming the fear loosens
its hold on us. And equally important, we discover that
others understand our fear, for they have experienced
something very similar. We are not unique. That knowledge makes it easier to reveal another fear, another time.

Perhaps the best gift I can give another woman
is talking with her about something I fear.
Naming the fear will help me. Sharing it
will help her because of the bond we will feel.

*Happiness consists of a solid faith, good health,
and a bad memory.*
　　　　　　　　　　　　　—*Clare Boothe Luce*

Resentments are guaranteed to hinder our growth. We
can never know full happiness when resentment clouds
our vision. Why is it so hard for us to "forget" the small
injuries of life? We have never been promised freedom
from pain. Many of the lessons we are destined to learn
will scuff our egos. But we will know happiness, completely, if we free our minds of resentments.

The formula for happiness is simple. We don't need
material wealth, a perfect job, or an exceptional relationship. In fact, it's possible to know happiness with no job,
very little money, and no significant other. Happiness is a
by-product of a healthy attitude. And a healthy attitude is
one that takes the normal turmoil of life and mixes it with
a belief in God's presence. The result is an acceptance of
God's will and a certainty that, in spite of appearances,
all is well.

*I am in charge of my attitude today.
Happiness is a choice I can make regardless
of what the people around me are doing*

Each of my days are miracles. I won't waste my day; I won't throw away a miracle.

—Kelley Vickstrom

It's so easy to forget to be grateful for our many blessings. We may take our freedom from the compulsion to drink or use for granted. Having learned to monitor our behavior and change it when necessary, we seldom treasure this skill as an asset.

The rut of complacency claims all of us at one time or another. And our complacency can lead us to the stinking thinking that's only a step away from drinking or using or some other compulsive behavior. Having sponsors point out our complacency may irritate us, but it may also save our lives.

Practicing gratitude will keep us aware of the small and large miracles that we have experienced on this recovery journey: We remember where we were last night (thanks to the clear vision of abstinence). We have reconciled with family members.

In fact, we are walking miracles, and God has a plan for the rest of our lives. Let's be ready for it.

I will try to be attentive to every moment of today, knowing that each experience is part of the miracle of my life.

It is important that we plan for the future, imperative that we accept an outcome unplanned.
—Molly McDonald

We sometimes feel confused over how to live just one day at a time while making strategic plans for the future. It seems contradictory to try to do both. Yet that is what a healthy recovery means.

Goals help direct our attention. They give us needed focus. They give us enthusiasm for making the most of our recovery. But just as we need goals to strengthen our resolve to move forward, we need willingness to let God be involved in our effort and, even more important, in charge of the outcome. God's role and ours, though related, are in fact quite separate. In our rush to move forward we sometimes forget to turn over the reins when our part is done.

We are learning the joys of living one day at a time. We are letting God be responsible for the outcomes of our endeavors. Each day in recovery gives us more time to practice doing only what we need to do and leaving the rest in God's hands.

I must let God take charge of the outcomes
of my efforts today. If I do, I will be
cared for in the most loving fashion.

*All shall be well and all shall be well and all manner
of thing shall be well.*

—*Julian of Norwich*

Why are we prone to exaggerating the seriousness of the
circumstances in our lives? Perhaps it's because we lived
for years barely on the fringe of sensible choices. We
overreacted to all manner of experiences, the mundane
as well as the momentous. Our reactions could turn any
situation sour. At long last we are learning a new behavior, but it takes practice.

As we learn to rely on a Higher Power to help us handle
our experiences, we begin to grow in peace and the belief
that all is well. Even when we are tormented by a decision, we can have faith that our Higher Power will lead us
where we need to go. Our part of the bargain is to ask for
help and to be open to guidance.

*I will know peace today because I will trust
my Higher Power's guidance in the situations
I face. All will be well if I do my part.*

We are giving birth to ourselves. Let's be mid-wives to one another through this difficult, yet exhilarating, process.
— Dudley Martineau

Helping each other survive the traumas of our lives strengthens us. We can't be overwhelmed by any experience if we rely on each other for support as we walk through it. What lucky women we are.

Having the courage to take advantage of opportunities transforms us. Where do we want to take our lives? Who do we want to become? The decisions are many and exciting. The counsel of our friends can guide us, but which doors we open is up to us.

Most of us experienced the pain of our lives alone. Revealing to someone else what our lives were like was far too scary. How could they possibly like us or accept us if they knew who we really were? Now those days are gone forever. Our decision to get help, and thus give help, is giving every one of us the new life we deserve.

My rebirth gives me opportunities to share
my good fortune with others.
I will be attentive to everyone today.

Learning stamps you with its moments.
—Eudora Welty

We never stop learning. We absorb information every waking moment. And while we sleep, we process what we encounter during the day. The conclusions we reach about these daily lessons will likely be based on the perception that dominates our lives. Do we perceive our experiences as for our good or for our undoing?

Since learning is ongoing, we are fortunate to have a more positive context within which to interpret our experiences. Alcoholics Anonymous and other Twelve Step programs offer us a set of guidelines to live by, which helps us interpret every moment.

We can anticipate what lies ahead, or we can dread it. What we learn from each experience reflects our attitude. Our commitment to the Twelve Steps determines it.

I will soak up the day like a sponge.
My education is within my control.
How lucky I am to have this program!

I wish I could keep in mind that God can provide,
God will provide, and God does provide.
                                                    —Marie Gubbels

Relying on God for the guidance to deal with our problems seems much too simple. We probably spent decades looking to alcohol, other drugs, and relationships for the solution to the ache that never left. We didn't know then that God was waiting in the wings for our prayers. Even knowing it, as we do now, hasn't prevented us from looking for help elsewhere, time and again. It has never been our nature to keep our lives simple. However, we are getting more practiced at the simpler life since becoming a part of this recovery program.

We may need to choose, daily, to believe that God can, will, and does provide for our every need. Because most of us haven't had a life-changing spiritual experience, we must decide every day to look to God. Fortunately, a moment of quiet and a tiny prayer are all that we need. God is never more than a thought away.

I will practice my reliance on God at every turn
of events today. I believe I will receive guidance
and knowledge concerning how to proceed next.

To stop behaving in a certain way is to risk the
unfamiliar.
                                                —*Jan Lloyd*

Old patterns grip us so tightly! Even when the behavior pinches us painfully, we are loath to give it up. Its familiarity makes it tolerable, knowable, somewhat manageable, and far less scary than trying something new. However, we are truly the luckiest women alive, because now we have a training ground where it is safe to try new behaviors. We can discard old, self-defeating patterns in the safe environment of these Twelve Steps.

We are on this recovery path because each of us wants a new life. We have grown sick and tired of the old ways that no longer work. And we have come to believe that change is possible if we look for it in the right place. This is the right place! At any meeting we can see other women who, like us, are trying on new behaviors and meeting with success. We are role models for one another, and every time one of us tries a new response to an old situation, we are all heartened and stretched a bit. We know that what another can do, we can do too.

I am in the right place today to let go of
the old and try the new.
My support is all around me. I will not fear.

*In my pain I seek the comfort and guidance of my
Higher Power. Grace and gratitude are the gifts
I receive.*

—Rose Casey

While it may be true that we grow from overcoming
painful experiences, we can grow without pain too.
However, we need God's help to grow, and some of us
are too stubborn to let God into our lives except when
we are in trouble. Thus pain opens our door to God and
growth.

Whatever way we come to know God is the right way
for us. The program offers no absolute formula, only suggestions of what has worked for other people. A quiet
time with a meditation and a cup of coffee gives some the
knowledge of God. A walk by the river or in the woods
dispels doubt for others. "Practicing the presence" or
"acting as if" we believe in God—these steps will, in fact,
give some of us evidence that God is here now. To try
these suggestions, we need not be in pain; we need only
take charge of what we think and what we focus on.

*My Higher Power is only a thought away.
I'll have the comfort and guidance I need
by "practicing the presence" today.*

Make lists; take action.
—Connie Hilliard

Our responsibilities can seem overwhelming if we let them pile up in our minds. Worrying about what needs to be done rather than doing it feeds our fear of inadequacy. We came into recovery certain that we didn't measure up, but if we use the program we can conquer those fears.

Focusing on "First things first" gets us moving in the proper direction. That slogan, coupled with "Keep it simple," can change how we respond to every challenge. We feel overwhelmed because we look at the whole, rather than at the individual tasks that need specific, manageable bits of attention.

This program and these Twelve Steps were created to help us stay clean and sober. But they can do so much more. They are a blueprint for handling every minute of the day, every person we encounter, every task that deserves our attention. Nothing piles up if we follow the guidance of the program's architects.

I will not be overwhelmed if I keep it simple today.
Doing one thing at a time is all that's expected.

The divided self exists in all of us.

—Marie Lindquist

One gift of sobriety is the growing awareness that we are complex, whole women—more than just our dark side. Defeated, we came into this program of recovery certain that our lives would be forever fraught with problems. Little in our experience made us proud. Surviving our hateful, painful, and confusing lives was our proudest achievement.

The moment we admit our powerlessness over our drug of choice and over other people, a fresh start commences. Becoming willing to let a Higher Power influence our lives gives us a chance to glimpse the brighter side of our being. We discover it was there all the time.

We'll always have both sides, the dark and the light. We're human. Nevertheless, we tend to strengthen the part of our "self" that calls to us loudest. Which side we hear is up to us.

*I am a complex woman. I have the next
twenty-four hours to live as I choose.
What actions will please me most?*

We are not unlike a particularly hardy crustacean.... With each passage from one stage of human growth to the next, we, too, must shed a protective structure.

—Gail Sheehy

Our passage into a new stage of development was initiated by our desire to stop using addictive substances. The values we lived by while using drugs no longer fit us. We need to shed our old skin and grow a new one that reflects our current worldview.

We are now, and always will be, in the stage of becoming, of trying to fulfill our changing dreams and aspirations. What we can accomplish at one stage of life is different from what we can handle at another. And yet an overall design is being shaped by all our endeavors. The more willing we are to shed yet another skin, the more centered, stable, and spirit-filled we'll become.

Do my actions fit my values?
As I outgrow my values, I will release them.
I will relish my growth today and
celebrate my new skin.

Blaming someone or something else doesn't help me to grow as an individual.
—Chris DeMetsenaere

It is not unusual to meet women in recovery who have survived harrowing childhoods or brutal marriages. Many of us have lived troubled lives and felt powerless to change the circumstances. If we continue to focus on those times, however, we will grow far less than we deserve.

What has happened has happened. We can't redo the past. Hanging on to it in order to blame other people for our failures and shortcomings builds a barrier to growth. With our minds on the past, we are not actively and consciously involved in the present, and this moment is all we have.

We are not responsible for the abuses others perpetrated against us. We are responsible for what we choose to do next. Being fully responsible, we will quit blaming others and make the amends we need to make. We will learn to pause before acting or responding to others.

I will feel empowered today if I accept responsibility for my every thought and act.

We're not here to lose our sense of humor.
—Richie Berlin

Being too serious is habit-forming. However, many aspects of our lives are serious and need to be addressed. Our disease, for one, is very serious. Working the Twelve Step program to the best of our ability is serious too. So are being honest and loving with friends, taking responsibility for all of our behavior, and being willing to change. But we can get in the habit of being too serious in many areas of our lives where a lighter touch is called for.

Cultivating laughter, so it too can become habit-forming, benefits us immeasurably; however, this may not be easy. Our family of origin taught us that some things were funny and other things weren't. If we were laughed at rather than encouraged to see the humor in situations affecting us, we may find it hard to be comfortable with anyone's laughter. But we can work on this. We can begin by spending time with people who laugh and see the humor in situations that affect them. Our families were our earliest teachers; we can pick some new teachers now.

*The more often I laugh today, the lighter
my spirit will feel and the healthier
my emotional life will become.*

Patience is bitter, but its fruit is sweet.
—Lida Clarkson

We all want life to unfold according to our plan. After all, we are certain we know what's best for us. But hindsight quickly reminds us that few, if any, of us had included recovery in a Twelve Step program as part of our life's plan. Yet here we are, and we are now more content than we've ever been in our lives. How did this happen?

We have come to accept that God has worked in our lives in spite of ourselves. We have been protected and guided all along the way, even though on occasion we stubbornly attempted to force open doors that were not beneficial to our growth. Fortunately, our Higher Power never gave up on us. We will fulfill our purpose with all the help we need when the time is right.

Remembering that opportunities come to us when their time is right allows us to wait and trust.

My patience will pay off today. I can be certain that what comes to me today is on time.

The expression of praise as thanksgiving, gratitude, and joy is among the most powerful forms of affirmation.
—Catherine Ponder

Praise inevitably has multiple effects. It positively acknowledges another human being, enhancing his or her well-being, while making us feel good. This offering of love, which is the substance of praise, heals all who share in its circle.

We can see the effects of affirmation in the women we admire. We can discern its absence, too, particularly among those who struggle. How difficult is it to give small acknowledgments to those we care about? Making a habit of this heals our own inner wounds too.

Affirming a friend or ourselves connects us to the spirit residing within. That bond fills in our empty spaces, making us whole and healed. Our security as women grows as we praise one another.

I will freely offer my love in the form of praise to the wonderful friends on my path today.

I walked across an open field at winter's break as the sun danced on the last few drifts. I imagined my fears would melt one by one as I learned to love myself.

—Laurel Lewis

Fear is as familiar as our image in a mirror. Although we have resolved many of the fears that bound us to old behavior, our original fears may have been replaced by new ones. Why are there so many things to be afraid of? New friends, old relationships, careers, family history, tomorrow…

Acknowledging our fear is the first step to getting free of its control. Naming the fear puts us in charge. Remembering that we have a loving Higher Power who won't abandon us, even in the midst of our deepest fear, can help us get through too.

But loving our small, scared selves will be the most nurturing of all. Mothering ourselves, in the way we may have longed for mothering in our youth, will carry us through the most difficult times.

Fears are part of living. They are neither bad nor good; instead, they can teach us. They can help us learn to love more of ourselves.

I will welcome my fears today.
They are my blueprint for who I am.
God and I will comfort me with love.

The self is a calm stable center surrounded by a continuous changing sea. Merge with yourself and be ready for any emergent sea.
—Coretta Scott King

Wise ones tell us to be true to ourselves. Being true to ourselves means daring to disagree with a loved one, even when we know it might cause painful tension. It means refusing to go along with the group's plans if our values are being ignored. It means standing alone, if necessary, in our family of origin if their expectations of us no longer nurture our growth.

With the help of the Fourth and Tenth Steps, we are learning who we are. We have recognized our shortcomings, and we have defined the assets that make our lives productive and enviable. Each day we are getting closer to knowing more completely the "inner woman" who is calm and centered. She is unruffled by the activity around her. She is quiet and accepting of the circumstances that have called to her. She is our guide, if we want one. She is our protector, if we need one. She is our voice when we become ready to let her speak.

I can be calm and centered today if situations get tense. My "inner woman" will take my hand and give me the words I need.

*We do not have to get caught in the middle of
other people's issues.*

—*Melody Beattie*

Learning to respect boundaries, our own and other
people's, eliminates much of the stress that hinders relationships. Accepting the behaviors and the opinions of
our friends as legitimate for them allows our relationships to teach us tolerance and patience and love. Our
journey on this planet is not about "fixing" or controlling
others, but about loving them wholly, just as we want
to be loved.

We need other people. Our humanity is enhanced by
our mutual experiences. But we also need to let others
learn from their mistakes and their own experiences,
rather than to help them avoid what they need for their
growth. We hate to see our friends in pain. Our compassion is triggered when trouble trips them. But their journey must be inviolate. We'll only prolong their struggle
by intervening where we aren't needed.

*It's hard to back away when a friend
is in trouble. But telling her I love and support
her may give her the strength she needs.*

*I always have two lists: things I'm happy about
and things I'm not. It's my choice which list I
focus on.*
　　　　　　　　　　　　　　　　　—Anne Arthur

Why do we all too eagerly see the glass as half empty
rather than as half full? It need not be a habit that we
are stuck with forever. All of us feel helpless at times to
change our vision of life. Discouragement and self-pity
become comfortable, and we fear that discarding them
will leave us vulnerable.

Seeing the glass as half empty is a sign that our attitude
is holding us back. Unfortunately, a bad attitude is seductive. It's as though we find pleasure, perverse though it
may be, in feeling sorry for ourselves. Sometimes we even
imagine staying in that place forever. It's then that we
need the warmth of loving friends, and it's no accident
that we are surrounded by them in this fellowship.

We may, at first, try to ignore those reaching toward us,
but we will soon feel their presence. We can thank God
for the inspiration to adjust our attitude.

*If I reach out lovingly to someone else today,
I will not need a nudge from my
Higher Power to adjust my attitude.*

Comparing my insides to other people's outsides causes me problems.
                                                    —Joan Rohde

For most of our lives we felt inferior. Other women seemed smarter, wittier, and more attractive. We felt inadequate every time we compared ourselves to other women. Getting sober hasn't freed us from this behavior, at least not completely. Fortunately, we now have tools that we can use in changing behaviors that hinder our growth.

Talking with a sponsor, sharing with a friend, or asking God for help frees us from the hold of negative behaviors. Comparing ourselves to others doesn't have to shame us any longer. All that's necessary is to stop the thought, think instead of God's presence within, and quietly bless ourselves and the woman who unknowingly triggered our reaction. Our progress in changing this shortcoming will be as swift as our decision to take this simple action.

I am in control of my thoughts.
God will help me every time I start to
compare myself to someone else today.

*People have always wanted to talk to me about
their problems. I guess I'm a good listener. Maybe
I have something to contribute after all.*
                                        —JoAnn Reed

No one is without value in this life. Maybe we haven't
discovered our unique purpose or special gifts, but we
each have a place in the universe, or we wouldn't be here.

Each of us can offer friends a valuable gift every day—
we can listen. Messages from our Higher Power often
come through the words of others. We perform a wonderful service for our companions by listening and by sharing our own experience and advice.

Rapt attention—giving it and receiving it—is perhaps
the most valuable contribution any of us can make. Let's
never underestimate the sacredness of listening.

*I will keep my own mind quiet if a friend wants
to share her concerns today. That way, my heart
may be able to offer her the wisdom she needs.*

*I believe that every single event in life happens
as an opportunity to choose love over fear.*
—Oprah Winfrey

When our past is strewn with tragic and abusive experiences, it's not easy to recall events as opportunities to love. Yet today we are safe, and we have come to believe a Higher Power has been watching over us every moment. Through the principles of this program, we are learning to forgive and to trust that we will always be cared for.

We cannot change the past. What happened and how we responded helped carry us to this point in our journey. We can cultivate love, now, for the present. The people who care for us will support us. The experiences designed for our progress will come to us. Our Higher Power will never leave our side. We can be free of fear today, if that's our wish.

*I will not fear the events in my life today.
I am ready for them. They need my involvement.*

*Having loosened our grip on the past, we are free
to reach for the future.*
—Ann D. Clark

Every day of our lives we think of some situation we wish
we had handled differently. Perhaps we left a job we now
miss, disciplined a child needlessly, or responded rudely
to a friend. Our Fourth Step inventory abundantly details our many regrets, but the past is gone. We can't take
back the job or the punishment or the rude responses.
However, we can make certain the Tenth Step we do
every night is not filled with similar regrets.

Recovery has given us a second chance. Let's not waste
this gift by hanging on to what can't be changed. We all
know what we don't like about our behavior in the past.
That's all we need to remember when we decide how to
behave in the present. We won't be ashamed in the future
if we take charge of our present.

*Today is a new beginning. Whatever happened
in my past need not control what I do with today.
Today is mine to be proud of.*

Owning our story can be hard, but not nearly as difficult as spending our lives running from it.
—Brené Brown

Our Twelve Step program introduces us to the personal inventory. In this exercise of introspection, we come to know ourselves. We often don't like who we see, but until we have acknowledged *her*, we are unable to change the specifics of our behavior.

Blaming other people and the "unlucky" circumstances of our lives for all our troubles is deeply rooted in who we are. But coming to believe that accepting full responsibility for ourselves will empower us, even when we are guilty of wrongdoing, is a major step forward.

Looking squarely at ourselves and owning all of who we are may not make us proud, but it does make us honest and humble. We have to be both, first, if we ever hope to forge the qualities that will make us proud.

*Today I will reveal qualities that I like very much.
If some that I don't like surface,
I won't deny them; I will correct them.*

I can change only myself, but sometimes that is enough.

—Ruth Humlecker

Happiness is more fleeting for some of us than for others. We may ponder this notion but fail to grasp the reason. However, careful attention to how the "happy ones" go through life will enlighten us. We will note how seldom they complain about others' actions. We will discover their willingness to accept others as they are. We will see that their attention is generally on the positive aspects of people and circumstances rather than on the negative.

We can join the parade of "happy ones" by letting go of our need to change people and situations that disturb us. Even when we are certain other people are wrong, we can let go of controlling them. Doing this means changing ourselves, of course. But this is the one thing in life we do have control over.

*I will change myself if I think something
needs changing today!*

My thoughts guide my day. Noticing how I awake
can help me save the day.
                                        —Kelley Vickstrom

We may envy friends who seem happy and peaceful.
Why aren't they troubled as we so often are? The fact is,
we can take actions to become more content too. One
of the simplest is to ask our Higher Power for a positive
attitude before we even throw back the bed covers.

Being in charge of what we dwell on is easier than we
might imagine. We can practice the art of focusing our
minds on the positive. Begin by stopping a thought, any
thought, in midsentence. Think, instead, of how lucky we
are to be in recovery. Focus on a blessing that is obvious
today. Any time an unhealthy thought surfaces, drop it,
replacing it with a blessing. This can become a way of life
if we make the choice.

We have felt enough pain and experienced enough
harm. Today can be much better. And it will be, if we
carefully select our thoughts.

I am as happy as I truly want to be today.
No one can steal peacefulness from me
if that's what I really want

Imagine
living in your head, untrue to your heart.
Imagine
the pain of separation.
Imagine
the depth of the longing for peace.
—G. Carol

Before finding recovery as a way of life, many of us barely hung on from one pain-filled moment to another. We incessantly tried to figure out what was wrong with our lives. We feared everything: our coworkers, our neighbors, the long days, the new experiences, the many strangers who crossed our paths. Miraculously, we were led to this program.

We can experience the joy of peace each time we remember to turn our will and lives over to the care of our loving God. To receive this goodness, we need only an open heart and a willingness to listen for the guidance of God. This guidance may come to us through a special passage in a book, through the words of a friend, or in other ways. If we believe that the guidance will come, we will hear it.

I want to know God's will for me today.
I will be attentive every moment.

Establishing goals and following through on them
help women build self-confidence.

—*Sharon Walters*

Alcohol and other drugs created the illusion of confidence for many of us before our recovery. Some of us held prominent positions in corporations. Others of us raised children and held jobs too. All of us took on responsibilities that might have overwhelmed us had we lacked the false security that drugs could offer. But their time ran out. Luckily for us, their time ran out.

Since giving up our drugs, we have had to develop new ways to build confidence. Fortunately, having this program and the Steps as guides, we have been able to make progress. The confidence we are building now through reliance on our Higher Power is substantive and real, not illusionary and temporary. We are learning who we are through our inventories, and that has made it possible to determine what we want to do with our lives. Our goals and our ability to follow through on plans are manifestations of our hard work. Self-confidence is the lasting reward.

My confidence will not waver today if I remember
to let God help me handle each responsibility.

FEBRUARY

There is no greater joy than to see my baby's face break out in a smile. It reminds me of the significance we have in each other's lives.

—Mary Larson

We have heard, over and over, that there are no accidents in this life. But what does that really mean? Can it mean that the pain we felt when a special relationship ended was intentional? Can it mean that the illness of a friend was God's will? Can it mean the promotion we failed to get was God's plan too? We can spend a lot of valuable time trying to figure out the real reason behind any set of circumstances, and we'll only be spinning our wheels.

How we respond to these situations is what causes the pain or confusion. When we learn to trust that God initiates our experiences, we will begin to know freedom from fear and confusion.

Every day we will have opportunities to increase our understanding of God's presence in our lives. The smiles we give and get are not accidental; they are part of the divine plan. So may be the chaos. It's how we handle the chaos that matters.

Every person I meet today is in my life by design. What I give to or learn from others helps each of us to grow.

My Higher Power takes many forms. One of the most comforting is the presence of the Great Mother, the magnificent Goddess who has a personal interest in guiding my life.
—Rita Casey

One of the first things we learn in this recovery program is that we have a Higher Power. Next we learn that we can define our Higher Power according to our own needs. As we change and get more comfortable in our recovery, our definition of a Higher Power, or God, may change too. However, wisdom is our reward for believing, and any gender or form of Higher Power will do.

Having a Higher Power's loving guidance is perhaps the most blessed of all the rewards of this program. Never do we need to feel alone. Decisions will be easier to make when we remember to ask our Higher Power for guidance.

Knowing that we have a loving Higher Power who truly cares about our safety and well-being makes every moment of our lives more peaceful and secure. We will be on the right path if we look for the guidance that we've been promised.

I may not understand why I have received
God's grace, but my sobriety is a sure sign that I have.
I will let my Higher Power guide me all day long.

Edge up against your pain and give it a name.
—Patricia Benson

Dwelling on our pain is unproductive and can heighten our anxieties. However, we do need to identify the pain, give it attention, and then be willing to let it go. Naming it sheds light on it, preventing the pain from living in the shadows where it remains free to haunt us.

Life is never wholly free from struggle and pain. As part of the human community, we learn significant lessons, and our willingness to experience the journey may sometimes appear directly related to the amount of pain we have suffered. But letting our steps be guided by our Higher Power, instead of fearfully resisting that Power, will make our lessons easier to learn and our journey smoother.

When the pain-filled moments come, as they may today, we can remember to acknowledge them and give them over to the One who has all power.

Today I will recognize my pain if it comes,
and I will take responsibility for my part in it.
It will leave when I do my part
and let my Higher Power do the rest.

*Absolute miracles happen when I can trust
enough and be vulnerable enough to get honest
feelings out of my mouth to another person.*
—Kathy Kendall

Seldom do we know in detail what we or others need at any moment. All of us harbor desires and dreams, but they are frequently fanciful and motivated by our not-so-healthy egos.

Nevertheless, we want to grow, and that's good. We want to feel more secure in our journey. We will have made real progress when we have learned to trust that what we need is contained in every experience, every conversation.

We are miracle makers, each of us. Though much that happens between us seems unimportant, none of it is accidental. We can't be sure what information is needed by our sister travelers. We can know only that God has brought us together. If we share with honesty and genuine compassion, we participate in God's plan.

*I can trigger a miracle in someone
else's life today by being honest and
compassionate in every shared experience.*

Being quiet does not mean sacrificing productivity.
—Jane Nelsen

To be quiet is to be focused. When we are focused, we are generally much more productive. But our inner dialogue often interrupts our focus. How seldom we manage to throw our entire being into the present moment. How much more we might accomplish if we could do this at will.

Learning to be quiet is not difficult, even though it doesn't come naturally to most of us. We are used to racing around; it doesn't occur to us that life can be experienced in another way. Once we grow accustomed to slowing down, quieting the clatter of our thoughts, we experience a sense of peace: the knowledge of the spirit within.

How lucky for us who share this recovery path that we have the tools we need to learn quietness. Practicing the suggestions in the Eleventh Step will change our lives.

I will relish the quiet today. What I need to do can be easily accomplished with quiet focus.

*Take time for solitude. How else can you
contemplate the blessings of recovery?*
—Abby Warman

Is it human nature to focus on what we lack? We waste
many precious hours, hours that can never be recaptured, bemoaning what we think we deserve. While
it's true that what we get may not be what we want, the
circumstances that have come our way snugly fit God's
plan for our unfolding lives.

It's far more productive to spend our quiet times
acknowledging the array of gifts we have received.
Perhaps we need help from a sponsor or a friend to discover that we have not been shortchanged in this life. If
we always gaze upon others, comparing their blessings
to our own, we'll never come to believe that each of us
receives what is truly necessary to our personal growth.
We are where we need to be. Let's practice gratitude.

*I am grateful. I sometimes forget that God
is in charge of my life. I will remember and
pay special attention to the gifts I'm given today.*

To gain maturity I need to become acquainted with all aspects of myself.
—Maureen Brady

Learning about ourselves is often likened to peeling an onion. We've grown layer on top of layer, sometimes for the purpose of protecting ourselves. None of us came from the perfect home. We've learned there is no such thing. We've all experienced injuries—some physical, some emotional—and we've figured out how to handle these hurts and go on with our lives. To be really healthy, however, we have to unlearn many of the cures that seemed effective in the past.

Delving into our psyches to discover who we really are can be intimidating. Fortunately we have the Fourth Step to guide our efforts. Let's not lament who we became in our struggle to grow up. Instead, let's accept that we did the best we could. And with the help of this program, we can become who we want to be.

I write my script today.
Who I choose to be is in my power.
My past performance doesn't determine
my present personality.

What do we live for, if it is not to make life less difficult for each other?

—George Eliot

Always seeing our struggles as the fault of others is a good indication that we need an attitude adjustment. There is no better place to get one than in this program of recovery. The women around us and the Steps that guide us can help us discover the joy of cultivating a new attitude.

Trying to determine the grand purpose of our lives can be overwhelming and anxiety-provoking. As alcoholics, we gravitate toward complicating the simple. That's why one of our slogans is "Keep it simple." We can apply this to all our relationships. Asking ourselves what we can do to help someone else at every opportunity defines our purpose in life quite clearly. Moment by moment, we'll never doubt what to do next.

My purpose is to help someone else today.
If I think someone is causing me a problem,
perhaps I should address my attitude.

Prayer is not a science.
—Mary McDermott Shideler

Since becoming clean and sober, many of us are coming to understand the purpose and value of prayer in our lives. Our friends tell us that any words spoken in sincerity to our Higher Power serve as prayers. That's good fortune for women like us.

This means we have the freedom to pray in any way that satisfies us. Now we can talk with God whenever and however it suits us. We will be heard, always. We will be answered when the time is right. What an empowering opportunity! Coming to believe this gives us a respite from our incessant fretting over everyday concerns.

Prayer can be anything—a thought, a request, a conversation, a plea, a dream. Our honesty is all that's needed. Prayer is not mysterious unless we make it so.

Every thought I take to God is a prayer.
Today I'll be free of anxiety if I think
of God before every action I take.

Loving means moving my ego aside and letting my Higher Power send energy through me to others.
—Jane Nakken

We commonly hear in Twelve Step meetings that ego is the culprit in our experiences, but what does that mean? Isn't having a healthy self-image the same as having a strong ego? Not exactly; a strong ego is not necessarily a healthy one. But how can we tell the difference?

Perhaps the best way is to look at our behavior. If we are trying to control others against their will, the unhealthy dimension of our ego has taken over. Backing off, letting that person be directed by a Higher Power rather than by us, enhances the good feelings we have about ourselves. That's how a healthy self-image is developed.

I will love the people in my life today.
They are here with me now because
that is God's assignment for me.

*Learning to listen to one's own inner voice is the
last crucial step to wholeness.*
—Paula Sunray

How does our inner voice develop? Those of us who
grew up in violent families most often heard abusive
voices. Or perhaps we grew up in near-empty homes
where the absence of attention injured our well-being.
Almost certainly the voices most of us heard didn't
affirm us. But the voices we can now cultivate, with
the help of this program, will change us and make us
whole and healthy.

Developing the inner voice we want and deserve may
seem difficult at first. Luckily, sponsors get us on the right
track, modeling habits that will help us change our lives,
just as soon as we express our willingness. Becoming
whole is our decision, and developing a healthy inner
voice is our responsibility. Utilizing the program tools
assures it.

*I can listen to a loving inner voice
if I practice loving myself and others today.*

Each day is a "workshop." Let's remember to keep our minds and hearts open so we won't miss our opportunities.
—Dudley Martineau

Looking at every day as a workshop for more productive or rewarding living eases the dread of new or unfamiliar circumstances. Developing the belief that we will be given exactly what we need to learn will change how we meet every twenty-four hours.

Before recovery we expected life to be hard. Our jobs often felt like drudgery. Our families seldom gave us the affirmation we longed for. Friends were unavailable. What we felt we deserved and sought, we often didn't find. That was then. This is now.

It's a simple change in perspective to come to believe that we are given what we need from our jobs, our families, our friends, every day. Accepting this belief will influence the outcome of every experience. Our lives will never seem the same.

I paid my dues for today's workshop by committing to recovery. What I will learn is up to me.

Our inner journey is a transformative process. It involves becoming who we already are in essence and letting go of the phony in favor of the authentic self.
—Mary Norton Gordon

In years past, finding the right face to wear was our goal in any social situation. Quite likely we succeeded too. We were accomplished at reading the faces of others, discerning who we needed to be in order to please them. Our worth seemed dependent on pleasing them.

Recovery doesn't mean we stop pleasing others. Learning to love others unconditionally, thus inspiring joy in them, is a benefit of recovery. But pleasing ourselves is of utmost importance too, and we can feel good about ourselves only if we are living honest lives. That means wearing the face that matches who we really are inside.

Our lives become less confusing as we learn to reveal our true selves. When we stop trying to be the person we think others want us to be, we will find more time to simply love them for the person they are, and to love ourselves too.

I will please others simply by loving them as they are today. I can be honest and loving just being me.

y husband, four children, six grandchildren, and
four great-grandchildren are the most important
things in my life. I love them all.

—Thelma Elliott

Liking, let alone loving, those closest to us seems elusive at times, because as family, we seldom put on our best face for each other. We express our criticism with ease, but showing and receiving love has often been difficult. Yet coming to really love the members of our family, loving their faults as well as their strengths, will help us love ourselves. And loving ourselves is the primary lesson we are here to learn.

Some of us no longer have contact with our blood relatives, whether due to death, abuse, or other complex family dynamics. However, we all have people we consider family. Time is too fleeting and life too fragile to let our most important companions walk by unnoticed, unappreciated, unloved. Each person will benefit—but, even more important, our spirits will be lifted—each time loving thoughts guide our actions.

I will take time to notice the most important friends
I have, my family. Those people most important
to me will get my love and kind thoughts today.

Choices are not irrevocable.... They can be remade.
—Julie Riebe

Knowing that we can make choices about every circumstance in our lives fills us with awe at the breadth of our personal power. For decades, perhaps, we felt we had none. Life was bleak, and we were at its mercy. How thrilled we are to understand, finally, where our power begins!

We are learning so much from this program. At times we wonder how we survived for so long on so little understanding. Our condition felt hopeless, and because we took no responsibility for changing our circumstances, nothing changed.

That's true no more. Every day we intentionally make choices about what's happening in our lives. Some choices, like changing a job or confronting a friend, are big. Others, like deciding whether to exercise today or tomorrow, are small. Large or small, our choices allow us to decide who we are, and none of our choices are without significance. That's exciting!

I will choose carefully today.
If a change of mind is in my best interest,
then I can change my mind.

No one can make you mad, sad, or glad but
yourself.
—Anonymous

Blaming someone else for who we are reflects our immaturity. If we surround ourselves with people who model unhealthy behaviors, we will feel justified in avoiding responsibility. We'll never grow into the women we are capable of becoming until we accept full responsibility for our actions, thoughts, aspirations, defeats, and successes.

It's not as hard to be responsible for ourselves as we might imagine. When we make the first move to be fully accountable, the feeling of being overwhelmed passes. Knowing that no one can ever make us feel uncomfortable, in any situation or circumstance, gives us immense relief. It's akin to being given a new life, a new personality, a new future.

Knowing I will feel however I decide to feel today
fills me with hope and enthusiasm.

The child that lives in all of us is always willing to take the blame.
—Margaret Haigh

We sometimes wonder if all women feel as we do. How many times do we apologize for situations that go awry, even those we had no part in? When conflicts erupt, why is it so easy to assume it's our fault? When we fear we aren't adequate as women, it's a small step to accepting blame for every ripple in a circumstance. We become obsessed with trying to control the uncontrollable, and then we think we're at fault when we fail.

Mood-altering substances appealed to us because they temporarily made us feel good about ourselves. Because we're human, we don't always feel good about ourselves. But now we have friends we can talk to in the most intimate way and program tools that can improve our attitude. The longer we're sober, the more obvious it is that our attitude is the culprit. Changing it changes everything!

I am not to blame for anyone else's problems today.
Accepting blame was a habit.
Cultivating a better attitude can be a habit too.

The more I force things, the tougher my life.
—Helen Neujahr

Are we driven to control? Perhaps we wonder if trying to control other people is part of the human condition. We've probably surrounded ourselves with controlling people, particularly if our friends share our disease. However, not every person alive has to control, and that means we can lessen our stranglehold. But how?

Understanding where our need to control came from is a beginning. Most of us, at least before recovery, were insecure. We wanted to protect ourselves from abandonment, ridicule, physical and emotional harm. The only way we knew to do that was to insist others fulfill our needs. We strengthened, day by day, a trait that hinders us now.

What can save us is acceptance of the first three Steps. Ultimately, we can't control others, so why try? Turning to our Higher Power can relieve us of our obsession, and that Power, if we'll let it, will direct our every move. The solution is simple—all we need to do is accept the simplicity!

I don't need to control anyone today.
I am not insecure just as long as I let
my Higher Power take charge of my affairs.

I have come to realize that all of my fears are false gods before me.
—Mary Casey

Some days are free of fear: they flow smoothly with not a single tremor. What's different on those days? Without realizing it, we probably left God's work to God. Fears generally surface when we get too personally invested in the outcomes of situations and in the actions of people we care about. We get confused and think our well-being is dependent on them and what they do rather than on God.

Fear about anything is the same as denying God's presence in our lives. It's not easy to shake the fear from our minds once we have given in to it, but we can if we follow the suggestions of this program. Most of us have come to believe in a Higher Power. Remembering to rely on that Power is our best option.

Any fear I have today is of my choosing.
Dwelling on God rather than on the fear
will change every experience I have today.

A woman who maintains fitness in her life has earned a PhD in self-esteem.
—Anne Marie Nelson

The word *fitness* covers a lot of ground. It's related not only to how we take care of our bodies, but also to how we eat, think, behave, plan for the day ahead, and pray. Every avenue of our lives exists on a spectrum of fitness.

Our Twelve Step program can serve as our manual for fitness. For some of us, the decision to exercise and eat right is an easy one. Decisions about how we think and how we behave, however, may be more difficult and require more discipline. Fortunately, the Fourth and Tenth Steps keep us in touch with our individual characteristics. We can make conscious choices about which ones to exercise in every situation.

My fitness today is within my grasp.
The Steps will anchor me.

First forget inspiration. Habit is more dependable.
Habit will sustain you whether you're inspired or
not.
—Octavia Butler

We sometimes have trouble defining ourselves. Anyone who spends much time in our presence, however, can define us pretty accurately. Our habits tell our "story" quite readily.

Many of our behaviors embarrass us, yet we repeat them. But changing them takes more than wishing they'd disappear. It takes a decision not to repeat them and the thoughtfulness to find a replacement for them. We return to old behaviors more out of laziness than intent.

Those of us in a Twelve Step program have the tools to make this shift in our behavior easier. Doing a Fourth Step to look at the past, and frequent Tenth Steps to stay on top of today, gives us the insight to define who we are and who we'd rather be. Changing who we are isn't that difficult if we have the desire.

Any current behavior used to be "new."
It became a habit only with continuous use.
I can decide to begin a new behavior today.

The baby learning to walk falls a lot.

—Kathleen Rowe

We are developing new attitudes, new behaviors, new patterns for nearly every activity in our lives. We can't be expected to master them immediately. The commitment to make progress on a daily basis is quite enough.

We won't be perfect. Ever. The determination to keep improving is as close to perfection as we need ever come. The challenge is in the effort. The growth is in the effort too. We are in this program to grow and change. It will happen, sometimes in spite of ourselves, if we keep showing up to do the footwork.

Falling while learning to put a better foot forward is expected. The learning process is just that: a process. A little effort, one day at a time, will hone our new skills. In no time, we will look back on our old selves with disbelief. How did we come so far, so fast?

I may make plenty of mistakes today.
I can accept that I'm learning and moving forward.

Healing can occur when I see my family of origin as just a vessel to bring me into new spiritual growth, rather than as the predictor of all my life's work.

—Judi Hollis

Traumatic experiences often teach us the most. This surprises us at first: How could the pain have had value? How could God have allowed it? It's futile to ponder these questions. We experienced what was necessary to fulfill our life's purpose. We are doing so now.

Many of us came from punishing families. Our successes were ignored, our failures held up for ridicule. How we functioned in our families gave us opportunities to fail so we could then appreciate success, to experience pain so we could understand compassion, to know regret so we could nurture forgiveness. Our families educated us. What we do with what we learned determines where we go now.

Every day I am embarking on an adventure.
What I do with my experiences today can be
a positive reaction to what I learned from the past.

We will never hear anyone else's thoughts if we are only listening to our own.
—Cathy Stone

It's not a defect to think. On the contrary, we need to examine all the issues in our lives, evaluating very carefully what action to take in each instance. Many of us are still clearing up the mayhem that occurred because we didn't give enough thought to situations in the past. But there is nothing gained by constant self-analysis, particularly during those moments when God has sent a friend to share with us her story or perspective.

It's never an accident when another person discusses with us an experience she has had. God intends for us to learn from one another. We are students and teachers, interchangeably. When a teacher comes our way, let's put our minds to rest. Her words may supply the answer we seek.

I will be drawn to the people who have something to teach me today. I will listen first and think later.

No one can tell you which choices to make. We can only show you by good example.
—Jan Pishok

We are attracted to people who share their wisdom and their hope freely, to people whose behavior reflects consideration of others. We recognize the love that radiates from some people as they enter a room or speak to others. We are all creating examples for others in every move we make.

One of the first principles we learned about recovery was that this is a program of "attraction rather than promotion." Though we may not have understood the meaning initially, we now appreciate how valuable that principle is. None of us like to be told what to do. Even when we ask for advice, we seldom really want it. But we can willingly follow the example someone sets, particularly if the outcome was successful. Let's learn from the good example of others. Let's be good examples as well.

*I am someone's example for healthy behavior today.
I won't steer anyone wrong.*

Nothing is real until you are close to it.
—Joyce Wadler

Addiction kept us from being close to the people and the experiences in our lives. It's not that we weren't present, but our feelings, perceptions, and reactions lacked clarity and sincerity, because our vision was distorted by the substances that consumed us.

Living free of mood-altering substances brings us much closer to the currents running through our lives. Without the cloud of alcohol or other drugs we see who our friends really are; we recognize what our experiences are trying to teach us.

What do we gain from being closer? Our awareness of the presence of a Higher Power is heightened. We come to believe that each encounter is by design. We don't doubt that we have a particular investment in every experience. We trust that all is well. We know that God is in charge.

Living on the outskirts of life used to satisfy me;
I didn't know it could be different.
Today I feel my involvement and cherish life.

Solitude is my time to talk to myself. Without it I get dull like a bird without a song.

—Abby Warman

In solitude we rest and are rejuvenated. Solitude is a moment alone, with our Higher Power as our only companion. Why must we have solitude? Many of us came to this program having been isolated from others, perhaps for years. But being isolated and being alone with God are far different experiences. In our isolation, we often dwelled on the injustices we suffered. Over a drink or a drug, we wallowed in self-pity. That wasn't solitude. We weren't listening for the voice of our Higher Power. Now, in our alone time, we can hear it.

Withdrawing from the bustle around us for a few moments with God will quickly enlighten us. We will save much valuable time when we follow the suggestions, the feelings, we get from our visit with God in the quiet spaces of the day.

I will sing to God's tune today
if I take time to listen for it.
In my quiet time I will quiet my mind
and listen to my heart.

Faith and love solve many things.
—Phyllis Elliott

Most of the situations we encounter need not become sticky; problems develop, however, when we insist that outcomes meet our specifications. It's far too easy for us to forget to let God be in charge of every situation and outcome. Luckily, we have friends and sponsors who offer frequent reminders.

Having faith takes painstaking effort for most of us. Yet we will feel so much better every time we back away from a situation and let God take over. Then we will realize that God has a better solution than the one we were proposing.

Learning to love not only others but also ourselves takes practice similar to the effort we put into developing faith. Love softens the harsh edges of conflict, and when we act from a vision of love, we see every event in our lives more positively. Choosing love as a way of life eliminates most of the conflict that undermines our well-being. Having faith that God is in charge takes care of the rest.

Having faith and feeling love are my
assignments today. God can help me do both.
Each person I encounter will give me an
opportunity to rely on God's help.

The journey to a new way of life—physically, mentally, and spiritually—includes the joy of rediscovering a faith that had been lost.

—Louise A. Rice

What does it mean to have faith? How does having faith make our lives different?

Having faith doesn't make us into totally new people. Our pattern of speech may not reveal our newfound faith, and our daily routine may remain much the same.

But there are subtle differences. We tense up less often. We seldom experience excessive fear over how something will turn out. We enjoy more energy. We are more at ease with the people in our lives. We come to believe that all things are working out for the best, and we trust that we will be given the information we need to make decisions or new choices when the time is right.

Faith gives us serenity and frees up many hours that were previously consumed by tension. We can fill these hours creatively when we trust the outcome. Surely this is the program's best gift.

I will let my faith work in my life today.
Nothing has to upset me.

MARCH

*Recovery is an intensely spiritual process that
asks us to grow in our understanding of God.*
—Melody Beattie

God isn't defined for us in any Twelve Step program. We have the freedom to create any image that pleases us. The shaming God of our youth can be gone. Instead we can call upon a compassionate Higher Power for guidance in handling the changing circumstances of our lives. Listening to other women in our group share their beliefs about God makes us aware of how valuable the guidance will be.

Never must we handle anything alone. Never. Understanding this influences how we perceive every situation in our lives. Circumstances that used to baffle or overwhelm us do so no longer. Snarled relationships untangle, and God's presence is evident everywhere. The more we trust in the Presence, the more conscious we are of it. The more we believe, the better our journey.

*Believing in God's presence today will make
every experience rich with meaning.
I am not alone, now or ever.*

*As I recover, I am learning to detach with love
and mind my own business with dignity.*
—Kathy Kendall

Very few situations actually need our input. On most
occasions we can contribute most by observing or listening. Although controlling how others live and think may
still appeal to us, we are learning from our friends and
sponsors the wisdom of detachment and the necessity
for boundaries between ourselves and others.

Our desire to "help" friends make decisions may be
rooted in love: we don't want to see our friends get hurt
by making wrong choices. But the wisdom of the program
tells us that we hurt our friends more by doing for them
what they need to do for themselves. While this may be
hard to believe at first, we can learn to trust that it is true.

It is enough to live our own lives thoughtfully. We have
been given a second chance through getting clean and
sober. Now it's time to give our lives all of our attention.
Let's free other people to do the same.

*I have enough to do just to live my life today.
I can show my love for others best
if I let them live their lives too.*

*Time and again I have searched for you, not
knowing that it was me I needed to find.*
—Betty MacDonald

We may have spent many years looking for the partner
who would complete our lives. We were certain that
happiness was guaranteed when the search culminated
in the perfect selection. How tragic it seems when we
discover that happiness still eludes us. The search, coupled with the belief that someone else is our ticket to
happiness, has led us down many dark alleys.

We are learning now that finding our true self offers us
the wholeness we thought would come from our attachment to another person. The Steps will guide our self-
discovery. Through the Steps, the meetings we attend,
and the friends we make, we'll find our real self. Knowing
her fully, accepting her completely, will fill the void we
thought only another person could fill.

*I will pay attention to who I am today.
I will honor the whole of me. I know genuine
happiness can be found only in this way.*

I pray that my recovery be filled with dynamite and feathers. I pray that my recovery be filled with quiet laughter.

—Jill Clark

Some lessons in life are painful. We may wish they'd all be easy and gentle, but if they were, we might not understand their value. Occasionally our Higher Power has to get our attention; we feel the pinch when that's the case.

We deserve variety in our experiences. Our emotions are created to serve us, to teach us how to get the most from the events and the people in our lives. The invitation to respond with a less familiar emotion is a gift. It's how we discover the many parts of ourselves. Until we know all of ourselves, we can't really love any part of ourselves.

Praying for help to understand our experiences, praying for the willingness to appreciate the "dynamite and feathers," will give us the helping hand we need.

I will experience the calm times and the storms.
From both I'll discover my purpose.

*Time brings summer to a close as well as winter
to an end. Time ages the brilliant petals of flowers
as well as prepares new buds.... we can trust
that time will bring the good to us as well as take
away the bad.*

—Amy E. Dean

We can stop worrying. We can stop criticizing other
people. But we can't stop the passage of time. Let's be
grateful for that. Had it been possible to stop time, we
might still be in unhealthy relationships, perhaps living
on the edge of danger or in a blackout.

The passing of time not only moves us beyond the bad,
but also advances us beyond the good. We hate to let it
go. However, we need to move on and be open to new
opportunities. Life is ebb and flow. We'll have periods
when problems seem rampant. At those times it helps
to remember that "This, too, shall pass." All will pass
when the lesson has been gleaned. Let's relish whatever
this moment gives us and know that its time will soon
be gone.

*Time is my friend today. Each minute brings
to me an experience I am ready for.*

*All sorrows can be borne if you put them into a
story or tell a story about them.*
—Isak Dinesen

Sharing our experience, strength, and hope with others
in this program helps to clarify for all of us the miracle
of recovery. Telling another woman how we survived
the most awful of experiences lets her know that her life
is survivable too. It's not by accident that the founders of
AA stressed the value of telling our stories.

Each time we share an aspect of our own traumatic
past, its sting is diminished. The more we repeat these
awful truths, the less their hold on us. Our storytelling
lets our listeners know that their own experiences are not
so different after all.

What lucky women we are. No longer do we hide ourselves from others. Each conversation with a sponsor,
sponsee, or friend is an opportunity to lighten our load.

*I will tell a part of my story to someone today.
She may be helped by it, and
I will be freed from it!*

*There's a lesson to be learned in every painful
experience.*
—*Mary Timberlake*

We can learn from every experience, but we may not
perceive the full impact of the lesson until months of
other experiences have passed. In the interim, however,
our reliance on God to help us through will count as a
valuable lesson, one that we may need repeatedly.

It might be helpful to believe that every moment of our
lives is giving us something to grow on. Many hours in a
week go by almost unnoticed; thus it's difficult to realize
that they, too, were contributing something to our divine
plan.

Getting comfortable with the knowledge that we're
alive to experience God's lessons and fulfill our destiny
makes the problems we face more acceptable and less
painful. God intends us not to suffer pain but to experience the world's joys. Remembering that will lessen the
sting.

*I will remember that God is with me
throughout today's experiences.*

Change comes about when we stop trying to shape
up the other person and begin to observe patterns
and find new options for our own behavior.
——Harriet Lerner

Accepting that we can't change someone else affects every detail of our lives. Many of us have spent years frustrated, even frantic at times, trying to control the actions and the opinions of others.

At last we have been helped to look at our own behavior. What a relief to be rid of the burden of being responsible for others' actions! Focusing only on ourselves is empowering. Every day feels more adventurous when we take full responsibility for our thoughts and words, leaving to others what belongs to them.

Being personally responsible for learning new patterns of behavior is like teaching a small child how to skip. Effort pays off in time.

I will have many chances today to mold
my behavior to match my self-perception.

Believe the best in yourself. Then it is easier to believe the best in others.
—Mardy Kopischke

Most of us have struggled—perhaps for years—trying to see the best in ourselves. Our less-than-stellar behavior has muddied our attempts to focus on our positive qualities. We have always had them; however, it may require a careful inventory and our sponsor's feedback to bring our positive qualities into focus. Why is it so much easier to remember the actions over which we feel shame?

Many of us can't see the good in ourselves until we can recognize what it looks like. It helps to start by identifying the good in other people; then we can learn to identify it in ourselves. This effort will ensure us many rewards.

It's really not important how we go about identifying our best attributes. That we come to appreciate them is the goal. And the beauty of this is that by openly expressing our appreciation we strengthen the good in ourselves and in others.

*The contribution I can make today is really so easy.
All I need to do is focus on a positive quality
not only in someone else but also in myself.*

Today I will stop brooding—and start meditating.
—*Nancy T.*

The Eleventh Step suggests that we meditate in order to know God's will for us. Not recognizing how to do that at first, we mistakenly think that when we "shut up," we're meditating. But we eventually realize that quieting the mouth is not the same as quieting the mind.

To meditate—to free our minds of worries, snarling questions, and constant complaints—makes it possible for us to know the best step to take next. We are good at "getting quiet" (perhaps becoming sullen is a better description), but clearing our mind of all thoughts is not easy. With enough practice, however, we will begin to savor the meditative moments and seek them far more often. When that occurs, we'll find the serenity we have been promised, the serenity we observe in others. We'll also find we know how to handle those situations that used to baffle us.

I can figure out my next best move today if I quiet my mind long enough to receive God's message.

To experience a feeling is to open a window to our soul.
—*Sarah Desmond*

Recovery offers us the opportunity to really know ourselves. It surprises us, initially, to discover how unfamiliar we are with our feelings and our motivations. Alcohol and other drugs muffled most of what we felt and thought for much of our lives. Now meetings and the Steps are helping us foster an acquaintance with our true self. It's both fun and a little scary.

We don't necessarily like every aspect of who we are now. And most of us loathe who we used to be. But having the tools to peel away the layers of denial about the past and having the willingness to face our feelings are paramount to becoming who we'd rather be. What we're getting to, what's deep in our soul, is the person God knew we were all along. Having the chance to know our soul is a profoundly important gift. Let's gently unwrap it.

I will respect all my feelings today. They tell me important things I need to know about myself.

The subconscious . . . works to create the reality
according to the programming it has been fed.
—Susan Smith Jones

The mind is seldom quiet. Even when we don't think we are thinking, we are. Our lives reflect our thoughts. It should be obvious that the way to get a better life is to think better thoughts. If it's that easy, why don't we have more productive, joy-filled lives?

As youngsters we learned to interpret the faces and the comments of those close to us. That helped us determine how to evaluate ourselves. If we received a glut of criticism when we were young, we may think poorly of ourselves as adults.

Just as the messages we heard in the past told us who we were, the messages we hear now do likewise. But as adults, we can now decide which messages to accept. Some we should cherish; many we should discard. We have the maturity now to replace them at will.

I don't have to accept how anyone defines me today.
I can give myself only positive input.
My output will reflect it.

I wonder what my life would be like if I were to focus my energy and thoughts only on things that really matter.
—Robbie Rocheford

We spend much of our precious time spinning our wheels. Our minds wander from thought to thought and person to person with no real sense of direction. Fortunately, we can develop the discipline of taking charge of our thoughts. We have merely to pause, quiet our minds, and focus. It's a technique that we can hone, and practicing it empowers us. It also frees us to spend our precious moments on beneficial ideas or activities.

Our attitude about a task will determine our approach to it. It may seem impossible to be in charge of our thoughts, but that's because we have never understood that we could responsibly and actively take control. Any negative thought can be stopped, even in midstream. And a replacement thought, such as "God is in charge," can be substituted. The exhilaration we will feel at realizing the power of this technique is astounding. Our recovery will be enhanced many times over as we grow in our reliance on this tool.

I will pause throughout the day to clear my mind. Taking charge of my thoughts will be enlightening.

Before I can become a significant other, I must
become significant to myself.
—*Kelley Vickstrom*

Why is it so hard to feel as if we matter? Putting other
people's wishes and needs before our own may seem
natural. We may feel shame when we say "no." As girls,
we may have watched our mothers and grandmothers
tending to the whims of everyone else. Probably without
ever being told, we simply followed suit. What's worse,
we may not have even expected appreciation for our
actions.

Now that we are learning to think of ourselves, we feel
a bit selfish. However, we must begin to honor our significance, and we have to understand that to do so is not
egotistical. In order to lovingly appreciate others in our
lives, to treat them as significant, we have to value our
own significance. Our Higher Power considers us significant; it's time we followed suit.

Affirming my own significance
will help me appreciate other people.
Today I will value my interactions with others.

*My intuition can lead me in the right direction
when my will and God's will are one.*

—Kathy McGraw

Sometimes we mistake ego for intuition. Then we wonder why doors don't open. We may try to force circumstances to meet our expectations. Our addiction led us to behave this way in the past, and this behavior helped to get us here to this program. Today we are striving for times when things do flow smoothly, when doors open at just the right moment, when we experience effortless living—in short, times when our will and God's are one. But how do we do it?

The key is to slow down and ask ourselves if what we are about to do feels right. Doing God's will always feels right. By contrast, being driven by our own ego often feels wrong, very wrong. In our using days we were adept at ignoring the feeling that something was wrong. However, our growth through the Steps makes ignoring what is wrong impossible now. That's good for us. And it's even better for the people in our lives. Wanting to follow God's will is the first step to actually following it.

*My ego is always ready to jump in where God's
will is needed. Today I'll slow down each time I'm
ready to jump, and I'll listen instead to my feelings.*

We are who we are, shaped and molded by the times, by the events, and by the persons we encounter on our way, and no one ever changes very much or escapes entirely from that mold.

—Ruth Casey

Everything we experience today is woven with all that has gone before. We are a tapestry in progress. We grow and change, heightening some of our patterns, successfully diminishing others, and maintaining still others. We need feel no shame for this person we've become; we've done our best. From this point forward, with the help of the program, our Higher Power, and the wonderful friendships that sustain us, we will add many new colors and stronger threads to the tapestry that continues to be us.

Even though there is often much we want to change in ourselves, there is much that will and should stay the same. Let's trust that God will guide our efforts in changing those traits that deserve our attention now, leaving the rest for another time. We have been loved, guided, and protected even though we are not perfect. That will be true always.

All that has gone before will help me handle whatever today offers. I am in God's keeping now and forever.

I don't always know what I want, but I do know what I don't want.
—Helen Neujahr

We don't want pain or confusion in our lives. We don't want friends to depart. We don't want a boss to be too demanding. And we don't want to lose control of the outcomes that are unfolding around us every day. There is so much we don't want. How lucky we are to be in this program and to have a caring Higher Power to help us handle the situations that we don't want in our lives.

We need the help of a Higher Power because we seldom know what is really best for us. Had we had our way in years past, we most likely would not be recovering. God had a better plan for us then; God continues to have a better plan for us now.

We must be ready to relinquish that which we think we want if the evidence confronting us suggests God thinks differently. We must let hindsight offer us enlightenment regarding God's better plan.

I will trust God to direct my thoughts and my actions. I will try to want what God wants for me today.

Through learning to like myself, I've been more
willing to understand others.
                                        —JoAnn Reed

Unrealistic expectations hinder our growth and relationships. We too often try to be superwoman, and we
want others to complement our drama. But no one can
match our expectations. It's helpful, then, to step back
and remind ourselves that we're all okay, we're good
enough. We are where we need to be for this point in
our journey. With effort we're coming to believe this,
little by little.

How do we give up unrealistic expectations, especially
when they are triggered by our shame over not being
perfect? Coming to believe that we are acceptable, even
lovable, to our Higher Power requires a suspension of our
disbelief. We must first "act as if" and then take time to
notice all the goodness in our lives. The evidence will
convince us that we are protected and guided, thus loved.
Meditating on this truth will give us permission to accept
and love ourselves. Understanding and then loving others
is only a small step away.

I want to love and appreciate myself
and all my friends today.
We are here to help each other.
God is here too.

With one foot in the past and the other in the future, how can we possibly know what new path we might follow today?
—Jan Pishok

Now is all there is. But how often, really, are our minds in the present? Honestly, aren't we much more focused on what just happened or what we fear will happen in the next hour or day or year? Being here, now, means giving up the past absolutely. It also means relinquishing all thoughts about the future. Occupying our minds with the experience of this instant only seems hard to do. We're far more used to greater chaos than what we experience solely in the here and now.

We have a direction that's right for us. Unfortunately, we miss the road signs because we are still looking over our shoulder at what we passed yesterday. The destiny we need, needs us too. Quietly focusing on our lives, one moment at a time, can assure us of fulfilling it.

Letting go of the noise I carry in my mind changes my life. I can feel and acknowledge what's here when my mind is open.

I can't expect you to share yourself if I can't do the same.
—Cathy Stone

We have been told we benefit from sharing our stories with others. However, most of us have shared intimate details of our lives in the past, only to have them repeated all over town. We may have decided that nothing was safe to share.

Now we are asked once again to share our secrets. What seems even stranger is that we're asked to tell them to people whose last names we don't even know. How crazy this seems when we first enter a Twelve Step program. Until we do it, however, we will not reap the benefits that are in store. We can only discover how like others we really are by telling them about us and then listening while they share similar stories. The intimacy that follows transforms our lives. Our time for self-disclosure has come. Let's rejoice and reap the rewards.

I will tell a trusted friend who I really am today.
I can count on affirmation and acceptance
if I choose my friend well.

*The willingness and courage to trust and accept
our feelings brings peace of mind and the knowledge that all is well.*
                                    —Abby Warman

There is no shame in whatever we feel. Our feelings
are products of our thoughts. If our feelings are uncomfortable, perhaps we should consider monitoring our
thoughts. We can always change them if they're causing us pain. It's important to remember that our feelings
serve as signals of who we are at the moment and what
we think about others. They serve us like friends, even
when we don't like what they tell us.

We came to this program for help to stop using alcohol
and other drugs. But that's only the beginning of the help
we are receiving. The other women at meetings and the
literature suggested as resources for growth help us understand how lucky we are to have an illness we can recover
from and a program that guarantees our well-being.

*I will appreciate my feelings today.
Whatever they are, I know that all is well.*

When we are all wrapped up in ourselves, we present a very small package to others.
—*Georgette Vickstrom*

Self-centeredness affects many people, not just recovering women. In this program, we are honing the skills that can free us from its clutches. Being willing to use these skills is the hallmark of our recovery.

Everybody on our path today needs our attention. Each person we meet may have something to teach us, or perhaps the reverse is true. But if we are focused on ourselves we'll miss these opportunities. Being open to other people helps us grow. If our attention is forever inward, we'll never grow beyond our current limited understanding.

Let's be willing to give more of ourselves to others today. The benefits we'll reap will move us forward in our personal journey.

*Today I can put aside my tendency to look
at every circumstance in relationship to myself.
With God's help, I can put my attention on others.*

Friends should be chosen carefully, because loving them will change our hearts and souls.
—Jane Nakken

We may not have picked our friends carefully in our youth. Many of us felt pressured to hang out with a crowd that didn't share our values. We frequently lived up to their expectations of us rather than our own. The internal conflict was painful, and we may still suffer from it. The blessing for us now is that we have the Twelve Steps to rely on for clarification and support of our values.

Having friends we can trust, friends who share our values, is one of the many gifts of this recovery program. We no longer have to feel different, isolated, or self-conscious because of our values or our secrets. We can dare to let others know who we really are, and we are learning they won't go away. Discovering the joy of friendships that nurture us helps us continue our careful selection of friends. Our youthful experiences with friends need never be repeated.

My choice of friends today
reflects the health of my recovery.

My children have a Higher Power, and it's not me.
— *Carolyn White*

We all have certain people in our lives, whether they are adults or children, who we think would fare better if they followed our will. Discovering that everyone has a Higher Power, one of the first lessons of recovery, relieves us of a heavy burden. It means we aren't to blame for what anyone else chooses to do. Of course, we can't take credit for their successes either.

What would make us want to assume responsibility for how others live? Surely we all have enough to do in our own lives. Perhaps our insecurity drives us to try to control others. We fear their actions won't include consideration of us unless we interfere. Fortunately, our interference is seldom successful. If it were, our lives would be far more complicated. Crises would be far more prevalent.

I will focus on my life and my Higher Power today.
Others' actions are not my responsibility.

I don't train for a marathon when I simply want
to run five-mile races.
—Patricia Roth Wuertzer

Our insecurity, our fear that we're inadequate, pushes us to overextend ourselves. We spent many years using alcohol and other drugs rather than fulfilling our dreams and aspirations. We may try to make up for lost time by demanding too much of ourselves now.

Making some progress every day is the best way to succeed at our goals. We'll discover almost immediately how good it feels to say we'll do something and then do it. But we must be wary of the compulsion to do too much. We're still addicts or alcoholics, after all.

Life is a process. Recovery is a process. Every day we get chances to learn whatever we didn't master yesterday. No one is keeping score. Let's ease up, make some progress, and leave time to smell the roses.

Today I'll remind myself that I don't
have to complete a big project every day.
Making some progress is enough.

*When we loosen our grasp on our concerns, there
is room for the spiritual essence of all life to move
through us in such a way that healing occurs.*
—Carol Sheffield

When we stay focused on a problem, we exaggerate it.
The solution can't reach us when the mind isn't free to
accept it. What we must do is develop the desire and the
skill to release all thoughts from our mind. Then and
only then can we be receptive to the spiritual solutions
that reside within.

This recovery program, with its Steps and slogans and
principles, can reeducate us. We are up to the challenge.
It's human nature to hang on to old ideas, old ways of
doing things. But we are growing, perhaps in spite of
ourselves, and our old methods don't live up to current
demands. It's time to trust what our sponsors tell us.
Release the grip on a problem, any problem. The answer
will come.

*I will not be caught in a problem today
if I am quiet and ready for the solution.
Stillness engulfs me now.*

To each particular person the world speaks a different, particular word and calls for a different, particular response.
—Mary McDermott Shideler

It's reassuring to hear that we are special. Most of us felt like failures for much of our lives. We lacked both confidence and enthusiasm. Occasionally we still tremble, fearing that we can't handle what's happening to us. However, we have been told that our experiences are unique and that no other woman could handle them in our specific way. We are coming to believe that this is true.

So many miracles are happening in our midst. The fact that we survived numerous dangerous moments should indicate that our work isn't yet complete. But what will we be called upon to do today? Can we fulfill this request adequately? Never fear. That we are here means we can. It also means that whatever is about to happen needs each of us, specifically. This is wonderfully reassuring.

I am invited to experience particular situations today. My presence is needed if I am called.

*There are many realities. We should remember
this when we get too caught up in being concerned
about the way the rest of the world lives or how
we think they live.*
—Natalie Goldberg

One of the most elusive truths we'll ever struggle to grasp is that everyone has a unique perspective about every circumstance, a perspective that reflects a personal understanding of the universe. We never doubt that truth for ourselves, of course. We simply fail to acknowledge that it's true for everyone else too.

There are times we can't shake the need to be right; our egos seem to depend on it. Unfortunately, we can't maintain any real peacefulness if we are always in conflict with others who have their own viewpoints. Winning the battle then becomes a painful victory. Believing in valid, separate realities is only difficult at first. But like any other opinion or attitude, it can become habit with enough practice. We have nothing to lose by giving it a try.

*I don't need everyone to agree with me today.
I only think I do.*

Inside me is a stirring truth that is guided by my
Higher Power. I am empowered by truth and joy.
—Laurel Lewis

Remembering that our Higher Power's wisdom and truth are as close as our quiet moments offers us welcome relief in troubled times. However, we must guard against hearing the voice of our injured ego instead of the voice of God. Many of us have for decades been led by our disabled ego. When faced with fear and discouragement, we need profound willingness to follow God's will rather than our own.

Having access to God's truth every minute of our lives can make each decision less frightening. No experience, regardless how unfamiliar, can be too much for us if we remember to listen for our Higher Power's direction.

As we strengthen our reliance on the Messenger within, we experience new levels of joy and inner peace. And we understand the real meaning of life.

I will listen to the still, small voice within
and feel secure and joyful, knowing
that my actions are God's will.

By embracing the unfair, I no longer feel fear or
rejection or lack of self-esteem.
—Eileen Fehlen

It's so human to quickly label an unwanted situation as
unfair and to assume we know what's best for us. We
reason that if God would answer our prayers, our lives
would unfold appropriately. It's also terribly human to
have to relearn repeatedly that God's will and God's
timetable don't always match our own; however, without fail, they serve us well.

Learning to appreciate the good in everything that
comes our way makes us courageous. In time few things
will fill us with fear, and that is measurable progress. We
were tormented by fear for so many years that we never
expected this rebirth of spirit. Life is beginning to feel
inviting, exciting, and safe. Let's step forth together.

I can be certain that God will give me
only what is right for me today.

Even on a rainy day, I can feel the sunshine.
Even when the clouds are gray, I can feel a glow.
There's a little light inside me, just keeps burning.
I take it with me, everywhere I go.
                                                    —Jill Clark

We carry within ourselves the single necessary ingredient for our happiness: a positive attitude. Nothing can ruin our day unless we let it. No remark can devastate us unless we let it. No unhealthy, negative attitude controls our thoughts without our assent.

Feeling good about the experiences we're having, regardless of their nature, is a decision. Trusting that some good will come out of every one of them is a habit we can form. We can acquire an attitude of hope for growth and positive change.

I will see the sunshine even through
the clouds if that's my choice. Today I have
twenty-four hours to practice this.

APRIL

*Take a risk. Being absolutely safe can also be
lonely. I might get hurt or rejected, but I might
also find a new friend—and that's worth a
risk.*
　　　　　　　　　　　　　　　　—Mary Timberlake

Having a Higher Power who is here to help us is the most
important gift of this recovery program. Perhaps for the
first time in our lives we no longer feel alone with our
fears and problems. We know that we can quietly ask
our Higher Power to walk us toward the solutions for
problems that have snarled our lives. We are learning
quickly that within each situation is an opportunity for
a lesson we have needed to learn.

　Whenever we fail to remember that God is with us, we
dread taking even the small risks of everyday life. Meeting
someone new at work or being paired up with a new partner at cards can undermine our confidence when we feel
alone and conspicuous. Being obsessed with how we are
being perceived rather than remembering that God is
always with us is part of our disease. Risk-taking, with
the help of our Higher Power, is part of our healing. Every
time we take a risk, we strengthen our willingness to take
another.

*With God's help today I will know a new level
of confidence and peace with each risk I take.*

The universe is made of stories, not of atoms.
—Muriel Rukeyser

Our stories give the universe depth, vibrancy, color, meaning. Yet we often forget our value to this planet, and we ignore the stirrings around and within us.

Most of us didn't grow up feeling appreciated. Our value to our family or to the universe was seldom celebrated. We just existed, and we did what we had to do with little understanding of how we fit into the big picture of the universe.

We're learning now that our stories, our presence, have always been necessary to the life of the universe. This gives us reason to pause and feel special. We may have been unaware of the life force around us, but we've always participated in the unfolding universe.

I am special, and my life, my story,
is a necessary part of the universe. That I am
here by design means I am watched over.

If there were no others to share ourselves with,
life would be meaningless.
                                        —Carlotta Posz

We often hear at meetings and from sponsors the saying
"There are no accidents." But what does it mean? That
wars are necessary? That a suffering parent is God's
will? That our disease is our destiny? We can worry ourselves sick over the answers, or we can accept these mysteries and try instead to appreciate the lessons they offer
us. It's the lessons that aren't accidental.

We are here for a purpose. We may not yet understand
what our contribution was yesterday or will be today, but
we can come to believe that the people we're living among
are necessary to the contribution that is ours to make.

We grow and change through our acceptance of the
unexplainable in our lives. The more willing we are to let
God be in charge, the more meaning we'll see in the small
details of our lives. Finally, we'll come to understand the
depth of meaning in those four simple words: "There are
no accidents."

I can trust that God is part of every detail
of my life today. I can either be peaceful
about what happens or be resistant and
miss my opportunity to contribute.

The Twelve Steps have powerfully guided me
from just surviving to living.
—Elizabeth Farrell

All questions can be answered and all conflicts resolved through our reliance on the Twelve Steps. Every relationship we have, no matter how insignificant, is enhanced when we accept the Twelve Steps as our philosophy for daily living. What powerful tools we have at our disposal!

The irony, of course, is that we resist using these Steps on occasion. We'd rather be miserable some days, resentful toward bosses or partners. Or we'd rather be obsessed with controlling a friend, even when our friend clearly wants, and will get, her own way! We mar our journey, give up real living, because we revert to our old selves.

What a blessing our program friends are at times like these. Their questions about our behavior can jolt us into awareness of how far we have strayed from the Steps that safeguard our journey.

I survived many experiences and lots of pain
before finding recovery. Yet I want more
than survival now; I want a real life.
The Steps are my guide today.

Loving, like prayer, is a power as well as a process. It's curative.
—Zona Gale

We tend to focus on ourselves too much. While we don't strive to be self-centered, we easily achieve it. And the more we obsess about ourselves, the less we measure up to our expectations. Then the shame of failure dogs our steps.

We can attack this condition from two angles. First, we can acknowledge our gratitude for even the tiniest of blessings: a reliable car, an inspiring book, a call from a friend. These small blessings help us to remember that God is always present. Second, we can intentionally focus our attention on the people we share today with. They are in our lives for a purpose. We can learn from them what we need to know about ourselves. What's more, we can be certain they are blessings from God.

My life is filled with the evidence that
I am lovable. God has not forgotten me.
Everywhere I look today, I'll see a gift.

We can say yes to life even at its darkest moments
if we can see it as part of the greater reality.
—Mary Norton Gordon

We glimpse only the opportunities that bear our name during any experience. We have heard many times in this program that we are never given more than we can handle. We can trust that this is true. We have also heard that God tells us only what we need to know right now; the rest will come to us when we are ready, when the time is right. That, too, we can count on as truth.

It goes without saying then, that every moment's experience is part of the bigger design for our lives, a design that always has a positive outcome. If we feel scared or confused by the changes in our lives, it's only because we have forgotten that God is in charge of the plan for our lives. We can say yes and be at peace.

I know that what comes to me today is a tiny part
of God's big plan for my life. I am not alone.

*We are likely to blunder from one crisis to another
if we haven't learned to act responsibly.*
—Jan Pishok

Before we began our recovery, we lived in perpetual crisis. Few situations unfolded exactly as we planned. We generally overreacted, and repeated crises were born. But no more, as long as we utilize the principles of this program. Acting responsibly means being in charge of our thoughts and our attitudes, which will avert the crises.

Surely adult women like us don't have a problem being responsible! But alas, that's not always the case. In years past, we seldom did the right thing. Now we may flirt with disaster because we let the addict loose in our heads. The tools we've learned from our sisters in this program can get us back on track, but we have to want to steer the right course. No one plucks thoughts from our mind or pushes ones in that we don't want. We're in charge, so let's accept the challenge.

*Acting responsibly is no harder
than I choose to make it today.*

*Silence should be used sparingly. But used,
nonetheless.*
—Stephanie Ericsson

When we want to control another's actions, being quiet is difficult. Our ego screams to take charge! When we bite our tongue instead, remembering the Serenity Prayer, we are spared an unnecessary confrontation. Occasionally quieting our mouths, if not our minds, promises big payoffs in our relationships with others.

Silence wears many guises, however. We have all experienced the punishing silent treatment from partners or friends. And our attempts to engage others in conversation are occasionally met with a silence that confuses us. Another's quietness may not be easily understood, but we must accept it.

Silence, particularly our own, is requisite to receiving guidance from our Higher Power. Being silent is often the most valuable action we can take.

*I will consider being silent each time an opportunity
to respond offers itself today. Doing the right thing
may well mean doing and saying nothing.*

Two new beings are brought forth during childbirth: a newborn and a mother.
—Anne Marie Nelson

Whether or not we have given birth to a child, we can certainly appreciate the miracle. The opportunity that we now have to give birth to a new self through recovery is comparable.

It is empowering to realize that we can create, or rather *re-create*, ourselves through the help of this detailed yet simple program. Who could have imagined that we, while in the midst of a chaotic, drug-infested world, were capable of taking on a new persona, becoming a new woman?

But here we are, charting a new course for our lives. Just as women need and deserve assistance in childbirth, we can rely on the help and guidance of other women who, like us, seek to sustain their rebirth. Together we will bring new women into this world, women who are eager to make a healthy difference in the lives of others.

I have the tools to create whoever I want to be.
I am an artist at work.

We learn from every experience, in retrospect,
that everything has turned out perfectly.
—Robbie Rocheford

We can all look back on troubling times and understand how they contributed to our growth as women.
At the time, we couldn't imagine how we would survive.
Terror and hopelessness were our companions then.
What relief the program has given us! We have a new
companion now. And we are growing in wisdom about
how perfectly our lives are unfolding. Every experience
is giving us new understanding and the strength to go
on. More important, we are becoming better prepared
to help other women survive similar experiences.

We are being guided on this journey by a Higher Power.
Each of us has a place to go, a job to do. Because we suffer
from "self-will run riot," we can take wrong turns. Then
we suffer the consequences. Fortunately, our Higher
Power is always close at hand, ready to help us when we
become willing to ask for help. This is likely the most
important lesson we are here to learn: ask our Higher
Power for help, and we will be shown the way.

I can trust that anything I experience today
will benefit my growth. If I ask my Higher Power
for help and strength, I will feel peace.

*I can have my way more often if I have more than
one way.*
                                        —Stephanie Abbott

We find ourselves doing battle with the world if we turn
every dispute into a confrontation. Seldom do any two of
us see something in exactly the same way. This diversity
is what makes life interesting—rich and educational.
If any one ego dominated how all of us perceived every
incident, life would be boring at best.

We all want our own opinion to dominate, whether it's
over when to eat or what movie to see. Perhaps it's merely
human to want our ego in charge. Or maybe that's only
true of people as insecure as us. In the program, at least,
we're in the right place. We can change. We can learn to
let others be right too.

There are many reactions to any situation. Our own
way will serve occasionally. We have the opportunity to
learn alternative responses too.

*There are many ways to interpret my experiences
today. I will be flexible and occasionally
look from another's vantage point.*

*Taking responsibility for the part I play in the
cause of my problems frees me to do something
about them.*
                                        —Kathy McGraw

We used to love to blame other people for the burdens
and hurdles in our lives. That someone else was to
blame for our personal upset was as obvious to us as
rain splashing against the windshield. Yet the longer we
looked at others rather than at ourselves, the more stuck
we became in old behavior.

We've since come to understand that we simply cannot
grow, we cannot harvest the fruits of this recovery program, unless we develop a willingness to take responsibility for who we are at every instant of our lives. As we begin
taking responsibility for our actions, we feel empowered.
We realize that we are who we have chosen to be. And
we will be who we decide we want to be. As that reality
permeates our consciousness, we will begin to know that
our hopes can become real, because the promises in the
Big Book are real.

*I will feel strengthened by claiming
responsibility for all that I am today.
Before taking action, I can pause and consider
whether I will feel good about my choice.*

The child in me says "Hold on"; the adult in me
says "Let go."
　　　　　　　　　　　　　　　—Harriet Hodgson

Learning to let go is growing up. Whether we're twenty-five or sixty-five, we have to learn to let go. We don't do it automatically. The principles of this program can serve as our guide.

Perhaps we learned in childhood that if we didn't want to lose our toys, we had to hold on to them. A pattern was set; we began hanging on to everything. But now it's time for new training, for learning to let go of everything: possessions, people, attitudes, opinions. Patience and practice accomplish the growth we seek.

We must be prepared for backsliding. Some situations cry for us to hold on rather than let go. We have to be vigilant and forgive ourselves when we give in to the old urge to control. Being adult takes desire and consistent effort. The child in us doesn't give in easily.

I have a choice today. I can handle all circumstances
as an adult and feel free, or my inner child
can trigger a confrontation. What will I do?

Letting go of old hurts makes room for new joys.
—Sefra Kobrin Pitzele

Dwelling on the painful past gets tiresome eventually, but some of us hang on to it longer than others do. However, seeing women move from the bondage of the past to the freedom of living in the present gives us hope. Once we let go of the pain, we discover far more joy in even ordinary experiences. That's the real surprise.

We have heard sponsors say that when old doors close, new doors open. Letting go of old hurts in order to appreciate new joys falls into the same category. Why not fill our voids with joys rather than recollections of pain?

None of us know how long a life we'll be blessed with. Accepting how tenuous life is helps us decide to seek more joy and less pain. The decision is only the first step, however. Taking control of how we think is the necessary action.

*I will experience more joy if I give less thought
to old hurts today. The decision is mine,
and I can make it and remake it if necessary.*

Work for justice. Struggle for forgiveness. Choose love.
—Patricia Benson

Justice, forgiveness, and love sound far loftier than they are. Developing these qualities requires only that we live as we think God wants us to live. It's as simple as that. Admittedly, when we have wanted to punish a significant person in our lives, we have often preferred "justifiable" anger or resentment over love. However, the emotional hangover that has followed the expression of our outrage has diminished any pleasure we might have gained.

Our inclination to forgive other people and ourselves, coupled with our decision to love rather than punish those who irritate us, seems to grow daily. Our changed perspective comes from our willingness to grow in recovery. We can be as peace-filled and as loving as we want. We're in charge!

I will stay in control of who I am today.
I can fulfill God's wishes.

Everything passes, and as I flow with this river of highs and lows, I become calm. I trust my experience and the life force guiding me.
—Ruthie Albert

Everything passes. There is perhaps no greater comfort when we're caught in the throes of a crisis than the knowledge that "This, too, shall pass." We lived many years without this knowledge as we struggled to change the unchangeable. Unfortunately, the only thing that changed was our level of frustration: it got higher. Now we know that we can patiently wait for a situation to pass. Nothing lasts forever.

The good times pass too, of course. We hope to hold on to them, but the same principle applies. The minutes tick by, carrying us to new experiences. What we need to learn will become known to us through both the good times and the struggles. They all will pass, having prepared us for the highs and lows that wait to serve us.

I am at peace with the knowledge that everything passes. My needs will be met today.

What thoughts are you willing to give up your happiness for?

—Jane Nelsen

Far too quickly we put the responsibility for our happiness on others. We pout and blame and cry, but our lives never change. This doesn't have to be true, however. We can decide to follow the example of the happier women we are discovering in this Twelve Step program. The difference between them and us is their willingness to be responsible for every thought they have, every feeling they harbor. It's a simple change in mindset, but it affects every aspect of their lives.

We are just as capable of finding happiness as any of the women we have grown to admire here. They have taken back their power from the others in their lives. They let no one decide how they are going to feel or think about a situation. They take charge of themselves. It's not all that difficult, or there would be far fewer successes. Let's try it today.

I can purposefully decide how I'll think and feel today. No one else's behavior will control my own

Our own gentleness is a powerful force in our lives. It is like the gentle flower that grows through granite.
—Patricia Hoolihan

We are attracted to people who have cultivated a gentle spirit. Their softness nurtures all of us who come into their space. We are soothed and made whole by their caring spirit. Let's allow our caring spirit to develop too.

The aggression we may have grown accustomed to in our families and neighborhoods need not claim us for all time. We have the power within us to chart a new course. We have examples of gentleness all around us; they are our guides and are here by divine appointment.

Whatever task we are destined to perform in this clean and sober life can best be accomplished if directed by a heart that cares. Being gentle promises each of us the same comfort it offers others. Each gentle act heals our heart and lovingly nurtures the future.

Being gentle today is much easier than being mean-spirited. My gentle side will nurture my inner child and remove my fears.

*I'm not very different from others. We all have
dark days of fear and doubt, but it's okay.*
—JoAnn Reed

The beauty of living a Twelve Step program is that we
don't have to dwell in the darkness ever again. We can
be free of doubt over the smallest or gravest situations if
we make the decision to turn our lives and will over to
the care of a loving Higher Power. To receive this gift,
all we need to do is ask for the help our Higher Power
has promised.

We begin to feel grateful when we develop trust in the
promises of this program. We knew fear and heartache
all too well. Feeling, maybe for the first time, real joy and
freedom from incessant worry is so exhilarating, energiz-
ing, gratifying.

We are given only the knowledge and information we
need for these twenty-four hours. But we can feel certain that the day will unfold according to the plan of our
Higher Power. We have nothing to fear. This day will
not be dark if we walk with our friends in this program
and let God lead the way.

*My day will be dark only if I shut out the light
of my Higher Power. Through my faith
and my friends I can know peace.*

*Now that I don't have to drink anymore, I'm glad
I'm an alcoholic.*
—Anne A.

Remember how we felt when we first heard someone say
at a meeting that she was grateful to be an alcoholic or
drug addict? We were astonished. We weren't grateful!
How much our attitudes have changed. Now we, too,
acknowledge the grace that has accompanied our addiction. And most days we are grateful.

We couldn't have imagined the lives we are now
leading. Without a doubt we craved more joy and security, fewer conflicts, a sense of belonging. But we never
imagined that giving up alcohol and other drugs was the
solution. We thought they gave us the only happiness we
deserved.

Now we are experiencing real happiness because of our
sobriety. We are willing to let a Higher Power help us, and
we are sincere in our efforts to change negative behaviors
and attitudes. Everything we need is now ours.

*Happiness is mine today.
It's as close as the expression of my gratitude.*

We grow in darkness and in light.
—*Marilyn Mason*

Every experience is a learning opportunity. Any abuse we suffered in the past, whether physical or emotional, taught us survival and resilience. Even though we felt defeated, we are here now, and we've learned to recognize relationships that aren't good for us. That's evidence of growth.

Sponsors tell us we are always growing. Even when it feels like we are going backward, we are growing. Recognizing our slower pace signals our awareness, and that is growth too.

Gone are the days when we doubted our ability to grow, to change. One of the first lessons we learn in recovery is that change is possible. Every meeting surrounds us with examples. And much of the growth has come through the dark periods of our lives. The darkness and the light have much to teach us. Every moment is to be revered for its message.

I am ready to grow today.
Regardless of the kind of experience I'm having,
I'll realize its worth to me.

*In celebrating the good in me that was always
there, I will continue to flourish.*
—Jill Clark

Dreading a Fourth Step is not unusual. We expect to confront nothing but numerous defects. However, we will also discover our assets. Our sponsors suggest that we need to acknowledge the good in ourselves to enhance it. Doing a Fourth Step inventory as part of our recovery will keep our assets fresh in mind.

If we put our mind to it, it's not difficult to choose one asset each day and focus on it during our encounters with other people. Practice is how we get good at anything. It's certainly no different when we focus on human behavior.

Maybe it seems phony to work at enhancing the good in ourselves. But let's accept the wisdom of our sponsors. Their lives have improved. If practice has worked for them, it can work for us too.

*Improving a small part of me at a time
isn't too much work. Cultivating my assets
in this way promises that today will be good.*

*To show great love for God and our neighbor, we
need not do great things.*
—Mother Teresa

We don't have to invent a cure for cancer or lift the burdens of a friend to prove our worth to other people. Being considerate of someone's feelings is quite enough, and it is something any of us can do. It takes only a moment's thought and the willingness to treat others as we'd like them to treat us. The real blessing is that we feel much better each time our heart guides our actions.

Loving others is perhaps the simplest of all actions we can take in this life. It requires no planning, no money, no muscle power, no problem solving. It's a simple decision we can make daily or hourly. Every person we encounter, every situation we face, is an opportunity for us to hone the skill. And every loving act or thought makes the world a better place.

It's human nature to treat others as we are treated. If each of us becomes willing to offer the hand of love to someone else today, we will indeed have done a great thing!

*I can make a worthwhile contribution today.
I can be kind to a stranger.*

Be spontaneous but not impetuous.
                                        —*Kay Lovatt*

Responding to the rhythm of the moment often blesses us with unexpected opportunities. Living in the present moment, rather than in yesterday or tomorrow, gives us our only chance for real growth and for knowing God.

Acting too quickly, however, without thinking of potential consequences, can cause extra problems for us. Taking advantage of an opportunity before it disappears doesn't mean acting thoughtlessly. Every circumstance we experience deserves a thoughtful reaction. When we rush to respond, we fail to hear our inner voice, which reflects our Higher Power's guidance.

We waste time when we focus on the past or future. Why do we complicate our lives so much? Thoughtfully experiencing each present minute gives us the gifts and the growth we deserve.

*I will return my attention to right now
every time it slips into yesterday or tomorrow.*

*Healing is learning to trust my own wisdom, my
own intuition.*
—Mary Zink

Being insecure is common with our disease. Some think
insecurity triggered our substance use. Yet it doesn't
matter which came first, the substance use or the insecurity. They were good partners for years. Unfortunately,
the partnership left us bankrupt!

Getting into recovery is like putting money in the bank.
Working the Steps, going to meetings, getting a sponsor,
being a sponsor, and taking time every day to commune
with our Higher Power are the deposits we make in our
account. When we hit a rough spot, we have something
to fall back on.

Believing that we can think clearly about the important matters in our lives is concrete progress. Our confidence about handling problems is growing. In time, what
used to baffle us no longer will.

*I am wise. I'll know what to do today in every
situation if I open my heart to my Higher Power.*

Many of us think that attaining status and financial success will make us happy.
—Helene Lerner-Robbins

Maybe we have to attain status and material wealth before we realize that they don't fulfill us. If we grew up in unhappy homes, we may have thought that material objects would change our lives. To discover otherwise takes wisdom, and we are only now seeking that.

The attainment of wisdom gives us the happiness we have sought everywhere else in our past. All that we longed for comes to us when we stop the rush to attain things and focus instead on the miracle of our spiritual being. Life is full of wonderful paradoxes; utilizing the tools of this program helps us discover them.

Let's not mislead ourselves. Having status and financial success doesn't preclude happiness; it just won't guarantee it. Finding God and settling for wisdom does.

I don't need anything special to be happy.
My reliance on my Higher Power
will give me lasting happiness.

*At times fear grips me, and I can concentrate
only on the anxiety. Then I realize I am in God's
care, and I need only trust and the fear subsides.*
— Michele Fedderly

Remembering God in the midst of a fearful situation is
often extremely difficult and at times impossible. But
when we can bring God to the forefront of our minds,
we sense immediate relief. Practicing reliance on our
Higher Power will strengthen our use of this profoundly
powerful tool. Our fears will be much more manageable
when the use of this tool becomes second nature to us.

As we grow in our understanding of this program, we
can look at fearful moments as opportunities to get closer
to our Higher Power. Many of us came into recovery with
little understanding of a loving God. More than a few of
us felt betrayed by God. We may still be like babies learning to walk. But our walk will grow confident. With time
and practice we will join the women who turn to God
for guidance throughout their day. And as a result, we
will know peace.

*I will let God help me in every situation today.
If I ask for help, I will get it. This is God's promise.*

God is the only constant.
                                    —*Ruth Casey*

Change is happening to us every minute. The cells in our body are constantly replaced. We are losing old hair and growing new hair every day. The plant world participates in a cycle of death and renewal every minute. We are surrounded by change. And when it's change that doesn't affect our egos, we accept it without comment, or in many cases, without notice.

Change in our personal lives is not so easily accepted. Losing a job can be devastating. Ending a relationship might feel unsurvivable. Moving to a new community, away from friends, can be profoundly lonely and disorienting. We haven't been promised unchanging lives. But we have been promised an unchanging, always-loving Higher Power. The most fruitful lessons we can learn are that God is with us throughout every experience and that change is introduced in our lives only when it helps us fulfill our greater purpose.

I will trust the experiences in store for me today
and have faith they are part of God's plan.

Unless our desire for human compassion is stronger than our desire to be right, to be secure or to belong, love will elude us.
—Marsha Sinetar

Knowing we are loved is what most of us crave. For brief moments we feel it; then it eludes us once again. Why does it slip through our fingers so quickly? One way of attracting the love we desire is to be willing to love others. What we give to others comes back to us. Unfortunately, we may give judgment, impatience, or anger far more often than we give love.

We can learn to give compassion. First we need to make the decision to be compassionate. Then we need to act as if we're comfortable doing this. When we have practiced it awhile, we'll discover that giving love and receiving the love we crave is within our grasp.

I will feel loved when I give love away.
I don't need to be right today. I need to be loved.

> *My life takes the course intended by my*
> *Higher Power when I go with the flow*
> *instead of against it.*
> —Kathy Kendall

The number of times we struggle today is directly related to how many outcomes we try to force. Our unwillingness to go with the flow can throw our journey off course. There is a rhythm to our lives—a pace and a direction—that's been set by our Higher Power. Until we come to believe in that truth and become willing to trust it, we'll cause ourselves many unnecessary problems and conflicts.

It's restful to believe that there is a plan for our lives. It takes away the fretting and the guesswork, leaving many hours for play and creativity. It also assures us that we are special, not forgotten as we may have feared in the past.

> *I am willing to believe that I am on a special*
> *journey. Today's experiences are part of it.*
> *I won't fight them.*

MAY

When I'm acting as if I'm the center of the universe, it's helpful to be reminded that I'm just another bozo on the bus.
—Rose Casey

Being "just another bozo on the bus" doesn't mean that our lives lack importance. On the contrary, we are coming to believe that each of us is here by design and destined to make a unique contribution to the whole of humankind. We are also coming to understand that our participation in an unfolding situation does not affect its entire outcome, crucial though our part may be.

When we can fully understand the meaning of this truth, we will sense a freedom that we did not know before. In the past we tried to be the center of the universe. This meant being responsible for nearly every circumstance affecting almost everyone we knew. Through the program we are learning that being in charge of ourselves, and ourselves only, is a big enough job in itself. Freeing ourselves of the burden of making decisions for everyone we love will enhance our well-being. Let's revel in our bozoness!

I am as free and as joyful as I want to be today.
I am in charge of myself and my well-being.

One of the many blessings or opportunities my
recovery gives me is the realization that there is a
bus out of the old neighborhood.

—Elizabeth Farrell

Today we have many opportunities to chart a new
course in our behavior. We don't have to keep feeling
inadequate or anxious. We can decide to change how
we act toward other people and how we respond to the
unexpected. It's our choice.

There is great hope and promise in knowing how personally responsible we are for our actions and, thus, our
successes. There is even greater hope in knowing that
we can feel as peaceful as we make up our minds to feel.
With our Higher Power's help, we are in charge of the way
we see the events in our lives. And with that help we are
in charge of how we maneuver through the moments of
every day. What lucky women we are! Never again will
we be at the mercy of our obsessive feelings. And never
again will life be any more difficult than we decide to let
it be. With the help of each other, our Higher Power, and
our willingness to change, we will know a new freedom.

I can hop on the bus of change at any stop
throughout the day. And it's a free ride to serenity!

*Sometimes the things that frighten you the most
can turn out to be the biggest sources of strength.*
—Iris Timberlake

Not many things would send fear through us if we remembered to rely on our Higher Power at all times. Yet we try to handle circumstances ourselves first. It's often only when we finally feel hopeless that we turn to our Higher Power for the help that awaited us all along.

We make our lives much more difficult than they need to be. Let's quit thinking through our problems alone, no matter how foolish they seem. Let's quit trying to handle tough people alone. Let's trust that every circumstance, no matter how small, is a lesson offered by God. And let's know that the outcome will be the right one for our particular growth at that moment.

Things that frighten us do so only because we have failed to remember the presence of our Higher Power. Let's pray for the willingness to remember God's presence. When we do, we will know a new strength.

*Today I will let God help me
handle every moment of my day.*

*To hear how special and wonderful we are is
endlessly enthralling.*
—Gail Sheehy

Sometimes we give in to others because we want affirmation. Belonging, however we define it, is important, and letting our own values slip often seems worth it. But there's a downside to this acquiescence. When we relinquish our integrity, we deny our very selves. And then we doubt our worth.

For many of us, knowing we are special has to be learned. Our families may not have conveyed this much-deserved message, so getting it somewhere was superior to getting it nowhere. But now we have the opportunity to seek affirmation from all the right sources.

Coming to believe that our Higher Power considers us wonderful just as we are requires that we dispel our more critical, though comfortable, self-assessment. This is the first step in finding the acceptance we've always longed for.

*Each time I doubt my value to those around me,
I will remind myself that God makes no junk.*

*My daily choice is to rise and shine, or rise
and whine.*
                                    —Anonymous

Complaining about every detail of our lives seems so
natural. We always have a preconception about what
"should be." Then, of course, "what is" is never quite
right. But it is possible to change this pattern of thinking. Contrary to what we may have believed up until
now, this pattern is made by us. It doesn't happen to us.

At first it may seem overwhelming to try to change a
behavior that is so rooted in who we are. And we'll continue the pattern many times every day, for weeks, maybe
months, before we break it. But the point is that we can
change. Every time we decide to respond positively to a
situation, we succeed.

Time, patience, and practice will make new habits
old ones. Willingness to try again every time we fail will
prove this to us.

*I will not whine today. If I start, I'll stop myself
and say something positive instead.*

Seeking strength from others prevents us from finding our own strength.
—Georgette Vickstrom

The principles of this program, the friends we have made here, our sponsors, and the contact we have with an ever-available Higher Power afford us valuable strength. However, it's important that we develop our own strength to complement what we look for in others.

Using the tools acquired in this program is a good beginning for cultivating personal strength. It's like growing a garden. We need to tend it daily, nurturing it, discarding the unproductive behaviors like weeds. When we do, we'll discover that the seedlings we're planting at every meeting are taking root and developing blossoms that signal positive growth.

I will be painstaking in nurturing my growth today.
My strength will be there when I need it.

*We all carry within us a very wise person, the
little child. To hear her call, to question her wants,
is to affirm her wisdom, to deepen our roots.*

—Margo Casey

Our inner child is helping us grow, understand, and
heal. She has walked with us always, though we may not
have been aware of her presence. She will be with us
forever, even when we fail to remember her presence.
Calling on her, we can gain the confidence and insight
we need to perform today's tasks and fulfill our dreams
for tomorrow.

How lucky we are to have learned of the presence of
our inner child. In years past when our struggles overwhelmed us, she was there, but we didn't know how to
reach her, how to listen to her. Now we do, and our lives
reflect our growing wisdom. They reflect our reliance
on her voice, which blends with the voice of our Higher
Power to become one unified guide.

We will never again suffer the struggles that tormented
our past if we stay open to the spirit-filled message that
is always just a quiet moment away. Going within will
assure us serenity.

*I will turn to my inner voice today and know that
all will be well if I follow the guidance she offers.*

If one is going to be truthful, one has to be very tender.
—Florida Scott-Maxwell

Honesty is always the best policy, right? We glibly recite that saying, but it's important to re-evaluate its meaning when we are eager to correct or direct the actions of other people. If being honest will unnecessarily harm them, perhaps being silent is better.

The program is helping us restructure our lives. We discover that many former, automatic responses no longer fit who we desire to be. That means we have to try new, less-practiced behaviors, such as being honest without being harsh or critical.

Learning tenderness is possible. With the help of this program and one another, we are learning to express the acceptance and love that have been given to us by our Higher Power. Giving away what we have been given is sharing the truth absolutely.

I will not hurt anyone today by any comment.
I will truthfully share the love and
acceptance I have been given.

Control is an illusion. It doesn't work.
—Melody Beattie

We've probably spent years trying to control the actions and the opinions of others. With powerful determination, we harp, we nag, we get angry and spiteful. Seldom do we succeed in getting our way.

Perhaps there are times when controlling others is appropriate. For instance, keeping our children safe is necessary. But we can't keep people from harm if they decide to take certain actions. The best we can hope for is that our suggestions help them control their impulses.

While controlling others is an illusion, controlling ourselves is not. We can and should be adamant about taking full responsibility for our every action, thought, dream, and plan. Our willingness to let others live their own lives will influence them in positive ways. That's almost as good as control!

*I will acknowledge how limited my power to
control is. Today I'll focus on my actions only.*

Life is for enjoying. It is not a race to see how much you can get done.

—Jill Clark

Before we quit using alcohol and other drugs, we wasted precious hours, days, maybe years. Consequently, we feel we must make up for lost time. We make promises and commitments we don't have the time or the energy to fulfill. This is a normal response to hindsight. After all, we missed many wonderful opportunities when our focus was on getting and staying high.

Making up for the past is different from making the most of each twenty-four hours. It's not how much we accomplish in life but how we treat others along the way that counts. We can accomplish our daily tasks while being kind to other people. But choosing the latter as the more important action will bring a far greater sense of well-being than trying to move mountains.

I will get done everything I really need to do today if I focus on being kind to those who cross my path.

*Once conflict has arisen, we are kidding ourselves
if we think it can be ignored.*
—Linda Riebel

Conflict is ordinary, some may even say necessary. And
it generally makes us tense, but that's primarily because
we want to "win" every disagreement. Through our role
models in this program, we learn that feelings should
not be stuffed or ignored, but they don't have to be resolved immediately either. Simply sharing with someone that we are angry about a situation is often enough.
Doing more often escalates a minor conflict into a major
confrontation.

Choosing to be peaceful, rather than right, isn't cop-
ping out, even though it may seem so at first. Rather, it's
opting to put our energies into positive exchanges with
others. Remembering that every relationship is given to
us by design, not accident, gives us reason to pause before
stepping on the toes of our teachers. Honoring them with
love and acceptance diminishes our need to be right.

*Letting go of my need to be right today
will truly give me peace.*

*I want to be loved, and for that to happen, I must
love others and I must want love for them.*
—Betty MacDonald

Feeling loved is so elusive. We savor the feeling when it comes, and we think if we hang on tightly, it won't leave. But we must give love away if we want to keep feeling it. That is the paradox. It is also a principle we can rely on absolutely.

Feeling generous in spirit toward others gives us a powerful blessing in return. We quickly sense that whatever we feel toward the friends and associates in our lives, we feel about ourselves. Carrying love for others in our hearts ensures that we feel loved too. It's easier to understand once we begin utilizing this principle. What we give away, we get back.

*I can influence whether or not I am loved by how
I treat others today. What I sow I will reap.*

The truest measurement of my growth and accomplishments is in remembering where I came from, where I've been, and where I'm going.

—Joan Rohde

Our daily routines can be so absorbing that we lose perspective on how we used to live. That's okay. We need to be present to the moment. However, it benefits us to remember occasionally what our lives used to be like. Never getting too far from the insanity of our past helps us be grateful for the gifts that have become commonplace now.

We've grown as the result of recovery. For many of us, very little in our lives looks or feels the same. We have new friends, sober relationships, more self-esteem, and a positive direction.

A true gift of this new life is that we have hope. We know we can do great things. We know we lived through our traumas because we had not yet fulfilled our purpose, our part of God's destiny. And we know we'll get the guidance we need to fulfill that destiny if we remain committed to the program's principles.

I am in a "growing" state of mind. My life is a rich and purposeful play directed by my Higher Power.

You can be anything you want to be if you want it
bad enough and are willing to work for it.
—Mardy Kopischke

Being anything we want to be sounds too good to be true. The key, of course, is being willing to work for what we want. Perfectionistic though we may be, it's still likely that most of us want to excel in every pursuit without the necessary hard work: Playing golf four times should mean no more whiffs. Being on the job nearly every day of the month should mean mastery of our career. There's a difference, however, between being perfectionistic and working hard.

Knowing that a hobby, a task, a sport, requires hard work shouldn't take the fun out of it but often does. We mistakenly think that we have chosen an impossible sport if we fail to demonstrate improvement each time we play. But we can learn how to do a task if we are willing to focus our undivided attention on it. Only then can we understand its subtleties. Only then can we be open to the help our Higher Power has promised.

I will be willing to work hard on every task
I face today. With hard work and the
willingness to practice, I will improve.

I have always been sort of quiet and kept my thoughts to myself. I have looked to "the Man upstairs" and he has provided the answer.
—Phyllis Elliott

Looking to one's Higher Power for guidance is a tool we are using with greater ease as we continue our journey in recovery. Many of us came into this program with little or no belief in God. Coming to believe in a caring God, one who will gently guide us through every circumstance, does not happen overnight. Fortunately, God is patient.

Trying to figure out how to live our lives—including what job to take, what person to choose as a partner, what opinions to have—was difficult when we didn't know we had a Higher Power to turn to. And, as a result, we made many unfortunate decisions. But making decisions today no longer needs to be a problem. For every situation we have the answer we need, and it rests with God. In the quiet places in our minds, we will discover what our Higher Power thinks is best for us. We can either follow the guidance or ignore it. But it will be there for us.

I will ask God to help me with the easy as well as the hard decisions I face today. Relying on God will make my life much more serene.

*To avoid pain at all costs forces us to reject half
the lessons life can teach.*
—Jan Pishok

If we could remember that every experience we'll ever
have is unique and offers us a lesson we will grow from,
we'd accept them all with far greater ease. What's to
be afraid of anyway? God is never absent. In fact, God
is present during every experience. Remembering this
makes us courageous as we walk through the turmoil
that interrupts the peaceful times.

Before coming to this program, we feared most of
the situations that called to us and understandably so.
We were often trying to do the improbable without the
wisdom or the guidance that might have guaranteed success. By taking the Third Step every morning of our lives,
as has been suggested, we can positively influence the
outcome of every experience we'll have. Hallelujah!

*I will not avoid any experience today.
I'll simply remember that God is present
and that I need to know what calls to me.*

An active listener is to be prized above rubies.
—Ruth Humlecker

Giving our undivided attention to a friend can be difficult. Even though we care deeply for her and value her friendship, we often find it hard to keep our own thoughts from intruding. As she talks, we take note of other people in the vicinity. We think about the tasks we have yet to complete. And we may pass judgment on what she shares.

Letting go of having these kinds of thoughts while in conversation with a friend is hard, but it's worth the work. No encounter is an accident, and every exchange with a friend or even a stranger has its reward for us. We are God's students every moment.

When we listen, we learn how to handle situations we might face in the future. We learn to show respect through our caring attention. We grow in our understanding of the value of friendship. Perhaps most important, we learn the value of cultivating a quiet mind. Only a quiet mind can hear the words of our Higher Power coming through the gentle voice of a friend.

I will be an active listener today. I am ready
to learn whatever God has in store for me.

It's all in the attitude!
—*Eileen Fehlen*

We are learning from this program that we are in charge of our attitude. No other person or situation can force us into a negative frame of mind. And if we have intentionally, though perhaps mindlessly, chosen to feel negative, we can instantly feel positive instead. A gentle reminder is all that's necessary.

Most of us got so used to negativity that we failed to see that we could feel otherwise. We resented women who always seemed happy and up. Now we understand, but understanding how our attitude is developed and taking charge of it are separate acts.

Being consciously and actively in charge of a positive attitude takes lots of practice. Every time we succeed in changing a bad attitude to a favorable one we become more confident that the next change will be possible too. We will soon discover that we are just as happy as we want to be. The power rests solely with each one of us.

I will be a happy woman today if that is my choice.
No one can make me feel otherwise!

My parents told me that I could do and be
anything I really wanted. I believed them.
—Molly McDonald

The encouragement we get from other people strengthens our willingness to try new pursuits. Unfortunately, many of us did not receive an upbringing that nurtured our confidence; thus we have developed a reliance on trusted friends to give us the gentle forward push. Our courage to take a course, confront an intimidating situation or person, or apply for a more challenging job is often borrowed from a friend. And that is okay. In fact, that is good. Developing a healthy dependence on others' honesty and sincere support deepens our connection to the human community.

The hand of a friend is a genuine blessing, a gift from one's Higher Power. We will each need a hand on occasion, and we will just as often have opportunities to help another woman find her strength, her power, to make a new start. Being ready to give as well as receive the hand of encouragement is God's will in action.

I will look for opportunities to encourage another
person today. My own strength and courage
will be enhanced in the process.

Ultimately, the only thing we have to share is our own vulnerability.
                                                    —Kathy Kendall

Giving up our secrets is the only path to the health and wholeness we deserve. Paradoxically, we're drawn closer to the women we admire when we talk about the parts of ourselves we abhor. We're really not as awful as we suppose. We're no different from every other woman walking this path. Mistakes, even the horrid ones, are human and repeated less frequently when the principles of this program guide us.

Each day, in order to strengthen the bond that heals each of us, we can let others know the person we are. By isolating ourselves because of our history, we deprive the women sharing our journey of the very information they need for insight into growth and healing. Conversely, by giving up our secrets we, too, can grow and heal.

I won't hold back my truth today unless it would harm the listener. Healing is what I seek.

*My sense of balance depends on my sense
of humor.*
—Joan Malerba-Foran

We're surrounded by situations worth laughing over.
Being human means making mistakes, and many of
them are humorous. Being able to laugh at ourselves
isn't all that easy, however. If we grew up in rigid, shaming, or abusive families, we may feel inadequate and
ashamed when we make a blunder.

Hearing our recovering friends laugh at themselves is
wonderful training for us. We learn by their example that
a good laugh takes the sting out of chaos. That, in turn,
offers a balance to our lives. Without some levity, we can
get far too serious and let every obstacle become more
than it needs to be.

Laughter not only gives balance to our lives but also is
healing, some believe physically as well as emotionally.
One thing is certain: few experiences appear too bleak if
observed through smiling eyes.

*I will be willing to chuckle many times today,
and I'll go to bed much happier.*

*When I take another's needs into consideration
and bend, I spiritually stretch.*
—Helene Lerner-Robbins

We have been told that this is a selfish program. Perhaps that has given us license to be inconsiderate. However, that isn't what the founders meant by a selfish program. While it's true that we must protect our sobriety always, it is never wrong to be kind and considerate toward others. Our kindness to someone else won't ever make us drink or use! That's what we must keep uppermost in our mind.

Along with helping us maintain abstinence, the program helps us develop a spiritual relationship that can change every aspect of our lives. Coming to believe in a Higher Power and turning to that Power for guidance and comfort allow us to experience hope in every situation. We can enhance our spiritual growth by treating others as we want God to treat us.

*My spiritual growth can get a boost today
if I get my ego out of the way and help
someone else feel better.*

*In order to become responsible, it is imperative
we take a close look at the effect our thoughts and
beliefs have on our lives.*
                                            —Susan Smith Jones

What's on our minds and in our hearts is pretty easily interpreted by the people sharing our lives. Our demeanor, our attitude, our expression, even our gestures speak loud and clear. The relationships we have with others mirror what is happening within ourselves.

Most of us crave control. We think we'd find lasting happiness if only others would do what we want. But wringing our hands over their independence won't change anything. On the contrary, addressing our own behavior, our own thinking, our own attitudes can encourage the very behavior we tried to demand all along. This is one of the tiny miracles that comes with working this program.

Taking charge of all actions, the loud as well as the very quiet, will give us the control we need—over ourselves and no one else.

*I will have the kind of day I want today.
My relationships will give to me what I give
to them in thought and deed.*

*But we don't know what we really want, so we
don't know where to look.*
—Mary McDermott Shideler

In vague terms we know what we want. We want happiness, serenity, agreeable relationships, meaningful work, good health, freedom from worry. But how do we attain these desires?

We may not have a detailed picture of exactly what we want, but in this program we never lack knowledge of how to proceed in any activity. Utilizing the first three Steps clarifies our next move. No situation needs to baffle us. We always have the program for guidance.

Before recovery, we looked to our drug of choice for our happiness and the solutions to our problems. When we didn't find them, we relied on relationships or jobs or food to fulfill our dreams. Again and again we were disappointed. We simply didn't know where to look for the help we needed. We'll never lack the knowledge again.

*I will look to my Higher Power and people
I can trust for guidance today. I know what I want;
I can find it.*

When I'm confused, I just try to do the next right thing.

—*Cathy Stone*

In the past, we eagerly sought freedom from our obsessions through alcohol and other drugs. We learned, after many harrowing experiences, that an altered mood didn't solve anything. The obsession remained. But there is a way to be free of obsession, and we have been selected to experience it.

Why have we been graced with recovery? We may never know. Many people never get the chance at another life. Because we have been given the chance, we may fear that it will be taken away unless we do everything right. So we obsessively worry. A good sponsor tells us that all we ever have to do is quietly ask ourselves, "What is the next right thing to do?" And then do it. It's not mysterious. A moment's contemplation clarifies what we should do. Doing it is all that's left.

Today I can live one experience at a time.
Keeping my focus small will never leave me
in doubt as to what to do.

> *If you have to swallow a toad, don't stare at it*
> *too long.*
> —Connie Hilliard

We have been blessed with a second chance. None of us could have expected to survive had we continued using alcohol and other drugs to excess. We were on a collision course with death, but the grace of God intervened, setting us down on this recovery path. The path continues to feel rocky at times, but we now have tools that promise us smoother traveling. We have to care enough to use them.

Attitude adjustment is a tool whose use we must all begin to master. Before recovery, seldom did we accept turmoil, no matter how minor, with a positive attitude. We were intent on forcing solutions or controlling those we thought we loved. Our failures fueled our drinking and using. Now our failures fuel our negative attitude. But we can take charge of our attitude. We don't have to love a circumstance to respond positively to it.

> *Many things will happen today that I won't*
> *necessarily love. I can accept them and cultivate*
> *a peaceful attitude, or I can pout and be miserable.*
> *The choice is mine.*

*We each need a successful experience in order
to grow in self-esteem.*
—Joan Gilbertson

What constitutes a successful experience? Far too many of us demand the nearly impossible of ourselves before we feel we are a success. Although we don't need a six-figure salary or an advanced degree to be successful, we may have been encouraged to set impossible-to-achieve goals, or we may have drawn up our own list of unrealistic expectations. In either case, we never saw ordinary achievements as success. Yet we are successful! Every one of us! It's our definition of success that is wrong, not our attempts to succeed.

We must redefine success and then count the myriad ways we demonstrate it at this moment. Success is staying clean and sober today. Success is thinking before replying to a comment or question. Success is showing respect to everyone around us. Success is sharing the program with someone in need today. Success is feeling gratitude for how far we have come. Success is trusting that our Higher Power will take us even further tomorrow.

*Each day gives me as many successes as I want.
My own actions will determine today's success.*

> *I guess I'm ready, or I never would have started*
> *down this rocky road.*
> —Jill Clark

Our past has prepared us for where we are today. Our fears often prevent us from believing this, but it's true nevertheless. As we gain trust in this program and in the truths outlined in the Steps, we'll come to believe that we are exactly where we need to be. And we'll know that we are in caring hands.

When fear of others or of the unknown overwhelms us, we have neglected to let the guiding principles of this program protect us. We don't ever have to feel afraid or unprepared again. We can share the experiences we learn from with another woman so she can grow too.

The rocks in any road are the gifts that push us to fuller development. Without them, we'd never become who our Higher Power has planned for us to be. Let's practice gratitude today.

I am ready for God's guidance today.
The difficult moments may be my
most important lessons. I will have faith.

Some days really are as good as a bowl of cherries.
Thank goodness I now know what to do with the
pits.
　　　　　　　　　　　　　　　　　　　—Sarah Desmond

Our attitude defines who we are and what we do with the tribulations that trip us. When we are confident or relaxed about the events in our lives, they usually unfold smoothly. On the other hand, when we are nervous or controlling, we can count on trouble. We get what we get in this life. What really matters is how we respond to it. Taking control of our attitude is all that's necessary.

We can't deny that some experiences are painful, even though they may be important to our growth. We don't have to like the pain, but the program invites us to incorporate what we learn from it into our lives. We can then share what we learn with others, so they, too, can be helped.

I can take what comes and make a blessing of it,
both for me and someone else. We learn and grow
by sharing our experience, strength, and hope.
Today is an opportunity for me and a friend.

You don't have to seek God in church. I find God
within my heart.
— Sandra Lamberson

Perhaps the most enlightening detail we learn in Twelve Step recovery is that God takes any form that suits us. It's not unusual to hear women speak of the Goddess who directs their activities. Others seek their Spirit in nature. Many of us still imagine the God of our childhood. Creating the image we want and a relationship that will sustain us is an amazing gift we receive from being sober.

Our sponsors say it's very important to find a God of our understanding. It's not unusual to enter the Twelve Step program with anger toward God, but we will be more productive if we develop a reliance on some Power outside of ourselves. The best thing to do is experiment with this new partnership. When you are faced with a situation you feel unprepared for, ask the God of your understanding for help. The results will amaze even the most cynical.

I will bring along my Companion today.
Together we can handle whatever comes.

Women, especially, feel caught between our
fundamental connectedness and a sense of
isolation. The challenge is to be intimate with
another and still remain true to ourselves.
—*Sherry Ruth Anderson and Patricia Hopkins*

Do we respond too quickly to the needs of others? It's important, of course, to respond respectfully—with love and acceptance—to others' problems. However, we need to decide what we can comfortably give while remaining true to our own needs. That's not always easy.

Why is it so hard to feel genuine oneness with others and to feel wholeness as an individual concurrently? A blessing of this recovery path is that we are learning how to do both. It takes time, though. And it takes willingness to be quiet and listen to our inner voice when the call comes to be there for someone else.

It's good that we desire intimacy; it's also good that we want some time away from the crowd. Including both, in a balanced way, is a special gift of this journey we make.

I will listen to my own needs along with those
voiced by my friends today. God can
help me decide how to respond.

JUNE

*Basically, I have two choices: either accept people
and their behavior at face value, or remove myself
from the situation. I cannot change other people,
but I can control my behavior.*
                                        —Lisa Keyes

Trying to control other people has been a long-term character defect for most of us. Becoming abstinent didn't take away the seduction of control. Perhaps for some of us becoming abstinent even heightened the seduction. Minds no longer clouded by alcohol or other drugs see with greater clarity many more invitations to control.

At first glance, it seems unfortunate that becoming free of the obsession to drink or use didn't also free us of trying to control the people and events in our lives. But had that been the case, we would have relied less on our Higher Power for help to grow and change. And the greatest gift of this recovery program is learning that we have One who is all powerful to help us make decisions, to guide us every step of the way.

*I will protect my serenity today by letting
the people in my life take charge of themselves.
If I begin to falter, my Higher Power will help me.*

*To not have control over the events that shape our
lives is difficult. To not trust that Someone greater
than me is shaping those events is unbearable.*
—Mary Larson

There is probably no greater frustration, particularly for
us recovering addicts, than the realization that we can't
control the events and the people in our lives. The insanity is that we try to control everything anyway!

The sooner we come to understand that being in
control only of ourselves is one of God's gifts, the more
peacefully we will live. What a terrible burden we've been
shouldering all these years trying to do God's work as well
as our own. Not having to be responsible for the successes
or the failures of everyone in our lives gives us hours of
freedom to explore new horizons.

Coming to believe in a loving God may take practice.
Yet the work is well worth our efforts. When the uncontrollable begins to frighten us, we can find relief in the
knowledge that God will take care of us.

*I will let my Higher Power handle other people
today. I will attend to my own business
and know many moments of peace.*

*I think it must have been at home, while I was
a small child, that I got the idea the chief end of
woman was to make clothing for mankind.*
—Lucy Larcom

We define ourselves within the context of our lives. We
may be single, married, divorced, or widowed. We may
be career women; we may be homemakers. We may be
in school or even retired. Our roles are multiple, but one
trait we share is the desire to live free of alcohol and
other drugs.

Our Twelve Step program allows us many opportunities to define ourselves. Drawing on the support of women
who care about us and the guidance of our always-present
Higher Power, we can redefine ourselves. We don't have
to fulfill another's expectations of us. Recovery is our
opportunity to follow our own path. Following our
passions while listening to the wisdom within is true
self-definition.

*I live with others. What they want of me
may not be my Higher Power's choice for me.
I will listen to the voice within me today.*

We're all recovering, all the time, from something;
we're growing out of the old and into the new.
—Jan Lloyd

We are in a constant state of change. With each passing moment we are gathering new insights, collecting new experiences, defining new perspectives. Even when it feels as if our friends are passing us by, we can take comfort in knowing that we are not standing still.

The rate of growth is different for each of us. It depends on how quickly we assimilate the growth experiences and specific information our Higher Power wills for us. The more we struggle against the closing of a familiar passageway and the opening of a new door, the more our pace is hindered. We can quicken the pace by trusting that we are always given exactly what our Higher Power has in mind for our next stage of living.

Each day's experiences are part of the trip that God has planned for us. We will never be in danger as long as we trust the spiritual guidance that speaks to us in the quiet places of our minds.

I am in safe hands. I can leave the old behind
and trust the growth experiences I will receive today.

*I empower myself when I choose not to be
a victim anymore.*
                                        —Kathy Kendall

During a rational discussion with friends, we easily reject the victim persona. We claim control over ourselves, and we definitely don't intend to give others power to harm us. However, when alone and faced with the bullies in our lives, we struggle to gather our strength and resistance.

Bullies come in many sizes and shapes, all ages and genders. They aren't always easily recognized. More often than not, they don't do us physical harm. But the emotional harm they wreak can be truly damaging. Their effects on our minds and spirits can immobilize us as severely as a broken bone.

Fortunately, we have the Twelve Step program to shield us from the abusers in our lives. It also gives us the strength of numbers. Sponsors and friends will help us remember to follow God's direction when we get momentarily led astray by the words or actions of those who'd harm us.

*I am in good company in my recovery program.
I will look to those I trust for support
when I need to stand up for myself.*

I will not take myself so seriously. I will let
laughter heal.
                                        —*Jan Pishok*

Being hard on ourselves is second nature to us. For some of us, it comes from growing up in a rigid, punishing environment. But the need to be perfect can be a self-inflicted wound too. We have suffered long enough. It's time to change. It's time to lighten up.

How do we break old, powerful patterns? Only with effort applied daily. Fortunately, there are exercises we can do that will help. For instance, we can make a habit of seeing comedies on TV, on the stage, or at the movies. We can choose to socialize with people who appreciate the lighter side of life. We can ask our trusted friends to help us see the funny side of our personal foibles. And we can ask our Higher Power to nudge us toward a humorous outlook. Perhaps the most powerful exercise is simply to make the decision to laugh more, and then do it!

Laughter promotes personal growth and health.
I will practice this prescription today.

*If I am a victim to everything in life, that is my
choice.*
—Peggy Bassett

Some days we choose the role of victim. We can't rationally explain it, but nonetheless it suits us on occasion.
Perhaps we're too tired to take responsibility for ourselves every day. Or maybe we have forgotten that we
have a Higher Power to help us. Luckily, since finding
this program, we settle for the victim role far less often.
It's not hard to call on our ever-present guardian angel
for strength.

Actively making choices that safeguard us, that comfort our healing hearts, becomes easier with practice.
Being surrounded by women who are doing likewise
influences and strengthens our resolve. Who would have
thought we'd come so far, so quickly?

Looking back on the past fortifies our hope and faith
that we will not return to that victim role so quickly.

*Being a victim fit me when I wasn't mature enough
to be responsible for myself. I no longer have
that excuse. The Twelve Steps will help me clarify
what I need to do to take care of myself today.*

In order to learn, risks must be taken.
—Ann D. Clark

We commonly took risks in the days before our recovery. In fact, every day that we used alcohol and other drugs, we risked our very lives, perhaps the lives of others too. Why then are we so tentative about taking risks now? Maybe we miss the false courage that our drugs of choice offered us.

AA and other Twelve Step programs can cultivate real courage in us if we want it. Remembering to rely on our Higher Power and our sponsors for support and guidance will help us take the risks that offer us growth.

Conscious risk-taking can be very empowering. We all deserve the self-esteem that comes with empowerment. Our lack of it made the addictive substances we tried far too appealing. We need never go back there again.

Trying something new isn't always easy,
but it is an opportunity to let my Higher Power
give me courage. I will risk it today.

When you least expect it is when you are
overwhelmed with the generosity of others.
—Iris Timberlake

Expectations can be both good and bad. At times positive expectations are appropriate and healthy. For instance, when we prepare for a job interview, it is far better to visualize in great detail a positive experience. This can lessen the anxiety we might feel in the actual interview.

In other situations, however, our expectations set us up for major disappointment. Maybe we hope a friend will acknowledge our birthday in a special way, but she forgets it entirely. In this case, expectations have done us an unnecessary injury.

Sometimes having no expectations is best. Then whatever happens can gratify us. At those times we can simply thank our Higher Power for blessing us as the divine plan has called for. It's these unexpected gifts that help us realize the power of God in our lives. We are being taken care of every moment, even when we are least aware of it.

I will be very conscious of my expectations today.
I won't set myself up for disappointment
if I'm aware of my thoughts.

*Pain and chaos in my life give me a chance for
transformation.*
—Carlotta Posz

Most of us are sharing this recovery journey because the
pain of addiction had become more than we could bear.
If the pain had been more easily tolerated, we would
have continued drinking or using other drugs, perhaps
for many years. Today we can be grateful for that pain.
We can see the daily evidence of what this new way of
life means. We are being transformed.

But what about the pain we feel when we fail to get
a job we want? Or the pain we feel when a relationship
dissolves? It's not easy to remember that these pains, too,
promise us growth and transformation. We may fail to
remember that our Higher Power is in charge and that
the sometimes-painful changes are part of God's plan.
We'd have changed very little if left to our own devices.

Trusting God to continue charting our course sometimes feels painful, but only until we remember that the
pain means God is nudging us into growth.

*If I am feeling some pain today, maybe God thinks
it's time for me to make some changes. I will try
to understand God's will throughout this day.*

I am learning to nourish myself with affirmations.
By adding a few short sentences each week, I am
able to create a repository of truths to draw upon.
—Laurel Lewis

Through our friends in recovery we are learning that
we have always been lovable, even though we may have
grown up in families where love was seldom expressed.
We have been told that our parents raised us to the best
of their ability, but that does not mean that we were
given the affirmations or the gentle guidance that we
needed as youngsters. Our parents were not able to pass
on what they didn't have, and old patterns die hard.

We are breaking the old patterns now. We are in recovery and learning to give ourselves the affirmations and
gentle guidance that we failed to get from our families.
We are sharing our personal stories and being loved for
it. We are getting the positive strokes we deserve from
friends. We are telling ourselves that we're worthy of
respect, love, and all the good that the universe holds.

I will create at least one affirmation today that will
help me move in a more positive direction.

I only have to be what I am, no more, no less.
                                    —Robbie Rocheford

Feeling that we are not good enough is common among women everywhere, not just among those of us who are in recovery. Often we wonder how we first got this feeling of inadequacy. We search our memories for experiences and people to blame. Other people's expectations, our shame, and the searing events of the past no doubt left an imprint on us. We are, unquestionably, the sum and substance of all we have known.

What we need to know today is that we are unconditionally loved and accepted just as we are, not only by the friends who surround us now but also by our Higher Power. We are learning to recognize the boundaries between us and those walking our path; this empowers us to let go of others' judgments and be more accepting of ourselves.

It gives me real joy to believe that I am okay.
By affirming this belief often, I will
imprint it on my mind.

Life is like an unbridled horse.
—Kay Lovatt

Many of us thought we knew where we were going after we finished school. We selected a path that fit our personality, we thought. Motherhood, a career, or both. Perhaps a single life or a low-stress job. Our friends suited our choices. So did our homes, our hobbies, our dreams. But then something happened. We didn't plan on addiction. Our drinking or drug use seemed social, at least initially. Where did the path veer? Why didn't we see the changes in store?

Life is full of surprises. Many are unwanted at first. But if we're willing to accept them as opportunities, we can discover greater meaning for our lives. Twelve Step recovery is one of those opportunities. Many new changes are ahead. We may no longer know where we are going, but we will get to where we need to be. Let's hang on and enjoy the ride.

I am on the right course even if I don't know exactly where it leads. I will let my trusted friends take the lead today.

*Spiritual growth is about confronting fear in
order to attain wonderment.*
—Jane Nakken

Few women have the profound spiritual experience
we all claim to want. It's more common to have brief
glimpses, now and then, of the tiny miracles that change
lives. Taking a moment to compare where we are today
with where we were a year ago convinces even the most
resistant of us that God's power is present in our lives.

We have survived broken homes, broken marriages,
broken spirits. But we're still here. And most of us are
healthier than we ever imagined possible. The torment
of fear that shadowed most of us for decades has been
replaced by faith in a Higher Power.

Going through pain, fear, and uncertainty with God
as a willing partner gives us cause to stop and relish the
wonder of this life, this moment. We're not alone, ever.

*Growing spiritually means I must talk to God
and trust God's presence every moment today.
That's a lot easier than walking alone.*

We can look at everything in our lives as having the potential to be either a blessing or a curse. Nothing, it seems, comes for nothing.
—Margaret R. Stortz

We interpret every experience in our lives. It's probable that we interpreted most past events as not in our best interest. But was that really true? What is more likely is that we resisted many vital lessons. And because of our resistance, events that were for our good troubled us rather than taught us. This recovery program can help us work on our interpretations.

We can learn from the terrible as well as the mundane. What may look terrible to us may appear sweet and inviting to someone else. It all depends on our perspective, and no one has charge of that but us. This program will convince us, if we'll submit to using it, that nothing happens without cause. What we do with what we are given makes all the difference in our happiness.

Happiness is in my control today. Whatever happens can be a blessing if I take charge of my feelings.

Don't dismiss your feelings, however painful.
They won't last forever.
—Abby Warman

Our feelings signal our thoughts. We have often said, "I feel depressed or angry or lonely or insecure, but I don't know why." It's not actually true that we don't know why. But we aren't always eager to take responsibility for our feelings, because when we do, we also have to take charge of changing them if we don't like them.

Twelve Step programs teach us that our thoughts always precede our feelings. This means that we think what we want to think; therefore, we feel what we want to feel. Thus we must acknowledge our feelings in order to adjust the thoughts that influenced them.

It's really not that difficult to change our thinking. It seems hard only if we haven't practiced much. The joy is that our feelings will follow. Painful feelings indicate painful thoughts. Joyful feelings follow the same pattern.

My feelings today are my indicator of
what I'm thinking. It's up to me
how I spend these hours.

Anger is a signal that a boundary has been crossed.
                                        —Niro Asistent

We don't always recognize where our boundaries or limits are. We may be unaware of others' boundaries too. In either case, our desire to please or control others can cloud our understanding.

Not having a clear sense of self-definition is common among women who are addicted to alcohol or other drugs. Most of us develop an unhealthy relationship with other people too. Because we simply want to be accepted by others, we may mimic the behaviors and beliefs of those around us and unconsciously cross the boundaries that separate us. We are frequently surprised by the anger that results.

It takes effort to define who we are and who we want to be. Watching what others do, how they respond, and then asking ourselves to follow our personal guide will educate us, on the spot, about who we really are, separate from the others around us.

I will know who I am, separate from others,
if I thoughtfully ask my Higher Power
to help me feel my differences.

We shouldn't blame ourselves for not winning a marathon with our very first step.

—Marie Lindquist

Perfection, as we define it, eludes us. Perhaps we've heard someone say that each of us is perfect as we are, but we don't believe it. After all, most of us don't measure up when we compare ourselves to other women. So how can we be perfect?

Unrealistic expectations pave the way for failure. Perhaps parents, teachers, or bosses had overly high expectations of us. The anxiety we felt at missing their mark may have taught us to feel incompetent. Sometimes we fear we'll fail even before we begin a job, a game, or any new challenge.

It's possible to come to believe that we are as good as we need to be. But it takes work. Our self-talk, meditation time, and prayers of gratitude for who we are can ease the struggle.

I am as God has ordered today. Doing my best is the perfect response to every situation.

Only when I have the courage to risk revealing who I am in heart-to-heart communication can I honor both myself and another.

—Mary Norton Gordon

When we hide who we really are, we can never trust that other people like us. We fear that if they knew all our parts, they'd reject or abandon us.

It's not surprising that we struggle with this. Shame-based families taught us to hide our feelings, our thoughts, even our hopes and aspirations. Not letting others know us became a habit. Unfortunately, it taught us to feel shame even when no shame was necessary.

Breaking out of this pattern takes courage and willingness. What's more, it takes constant practice. Only by repeatedly showing others who we really are and realizing that they don't go away can we learn the joy inherent in honest, intimate communication. Twelve Step groups offer us a safe place for mastering this skill. What lucky women we are!

I am okay, all of me, and I'll share who I am with friends today. Even the parts of me that need work can be shared safely.

.hings that happen aren't necessarily good or
bad; they just fit into my plans, or they don't.
—Anne Arthur

Because we are certain we know what is best for us, we seldom let our Higher Power take responsibility for the circumstances that capture our attention. More often, we map out what we think should happen, then spend hours worrying when the unexpected occurs.

It is normal for us to want our lives to unfold according to our dreams. Maturity, however, means planning for today and tomorrow, and remembering not to force control over situations that involve other people. And most of our experiences include other people.

Our growth in recovery can be measured by how quickly we let God take charge of our experiences and outcomes. By turning our plans over to God and acknowledging that greater plan, we signal our readiness for the serenity this program promises.

I am guaranteed a secure partnership with a
Higher Power. If I rely on that partnership today,
I will feel serene, and I will instinctively know
that my plan and God's are one and the same.

Often I need to cut myself and others some slack.
When I remind myself to lighten up, the intensity
of the situation diminishes.
—Lisa Keyes

Most of us have honed, quite skillfully, our ability to take most situations far too seriously. Perhaps if we were as careful to hone our skill of relying on our Higher Power to see us through situations, we'd more fully enjoy the moments God gives us.

Our struggle with perfectionism, coupled with our need to control outcomes, makes us experience life far too gravely. At the root of these character traits lies fear. We may not recognize our behavior as fear based. However, were we not anxious about unfolding events, we'd feel peaceful and free to pursue activities that would reward us with the spiritual growth this program has promised.

Being reminded to lighten up may irritate us and feel like criticism at the time, but this advice can quickly change how we feel. After all, what we want is more serenity in our lives. We simply need reminders about how to attain it. Lightening up is one of the best and simplest of reminders.

I will remind myself to lighten up today
as many times as it takes to feel some peace.

Even when you find out, you never really know.
—Julie Riebe

There are very few absolutes. Yet we can safely assume the sun will rise and the earth will continue its rotation. We can be certain that we have a Higher Power who has always loved us and will continue to. Likewise, we can be certain that the fellowship will always be available to us and that God will never give us more than we can handle.

Experience has shown us, however, that many things we thought we knew and could count on have faded before our very eyes. Opinions change, relationships end, circumstances develop, God's plan intervenes.

Not really knowing what lies ahead lends an air of excitement to our lives. Trusting our Higher Power to walk us through every experience means we don't have to worry about an outcome. Letting God be in charge promises us freedom from worry. This is an absolute we can count on.

*There is only one thing I need to know
today: God is present to help me.
I can count on this with absolute certainty.*

Growth always comes for me through struggle and challenge. I have learned it is worth the effort to gain insight and personal strength.
—Michele Fedderly

We seldom enjoy challenges while in the midst of them. Even though we have gained the wisdom to understand that they will have value to us, we generally fail to appreciate them as they unfold. Let's not fault ourselves for that. We are doing the best we can. From this program we are discovering a whole new way of seeing our lives, and it takes time to fully incorporate this new vision.

We are destined to grow—our "assignments" will ensure that. We can be certain that some of them will be difficult, at least briefly. We can be equally certain that our pain will leave us just as swiftly as we reach for the hand of a caring companion. We are not on this journey alone. Look around. Our companions are everywhere, and we can help one another.

I am surrounded by women who do want to help me today. I will receive support and guidance every time I ask for it.

Doing nothing is sometimes the best thing we can do.
—Connie Hilliard

Recovery inspires us to change, to move forward. We set goals and count on other people to support our efforts. Having a direction is significant to us because for years many of us floundered. Now we fear regressing, so when obstacles surface, we panic. We want to take immediate action, and we want others to bend to our will. On days like this, let's remember that we still have much to learn.

It's okay to sit out a problem occasionally. Not every conflict has to be resolved or even discussed. Many circumstances need no settling. Sometimes just quieting down releases us from a problem. And in its own way, that is a decision. We are doing something. When we understand that, we'll feel better about doing nothing. It will no longer feel like passive acceptance of a bad situation.

Often the wisest thing we can do is nothing. We have heard this advice many times at meetings and from sponsors. Let's follow it.

Before I take action on any matter today,
I'll ask myself if I really need to do so.
Doing nothing may be just right.

Inner hunger is a divine discontent that keeps us moving forward.
　　　　　　　　　　　　　　　　—Jacquelyn Small

We all want things we don't have. Even people who don't develop addictions are seldom content with what life has served them. There is a remedy for this condition, however: the Third Step. Coming to believe that a Higher Power is watching over us, ushering into our lives exactly what we need on schedule, relieves our obsession with wanting what we don't have. God will give it to us, if we need it, when the time is right.

It's not wrong to want what we don't have. The folly is letting our inner desires rule us, rather than trusting that we will be shown how to draw them to us if and when they become right for us.

Moving forward can be defined in many ways. Waking each morning to the thought that God has something new and unexpected in store for us is moving forward. Let's relish this thought!

I will be content today if I remember that my Higher Power has my day well planned.

*Addiction is our mind's attachment to a particular
substance or behavior in the belief that it is going
to create the sense of expansion that we crave.*
                                        —*Niro Asistent*

We are painfully slow learners. We repeat old behaviors and are surprised when the same old results occur. On the other hand, most of us swiftly learned that our return to using an addictive substance meant the same old trouble. Why can't we see the parallel here?

Perhaps we need to act as better teachers to one another. Let's concentrate on reminding one another that old patterns can't create new results; they keep us forever stuck.

We want to grow, to change, to feel whole. We wouldn't have come to this program had we wanted to stay who we were. We forget, that's all. But we can learn to remember, with one another's help, that nothing new comes out of something old.

*I want to be a good student and a good
teacher today. With my Higher Power's help
and my willingness, I can do both.*

We are all artists and our greatest creation is in the living of our lives.
—Dudley Martineau

When we hear the word *artist* most of us think of someone like O'Keefe or Chicago or Wharton or Dickinson. We certainly don't think of ourselves as artists. Fortunately, this program is able to help us broaden our definition of *artist*. Using these Twelve Steps allows us to create whoever we really want to be.

Many of us imitated some bad role models for much of our lives. We willingly let others define us. Perhaps it seemed easier than taking charge of ourselves and creating who we really longed to be.

But using the tools of this program, we are able to decide exactly how we want to respond to every experience today. We can be the women we want to be. As we stand before the canvas of our lives, we are free to create a world of joy and serenity.

I will look to this program and my Higher Power for guidance as I create myself today.

When friends say I'm their anchor, I am grateful
for the knowledge that I can trust them to sail
without me.

—D. M. G.

An important element of this recovery program is our
willingness to be there for other women. In the wreck-
age of the past, we seldom were. Our focus was narrow;
we were self-centered, jealous, and full of fear. Now we
can be counted on, at least part of the time. Being a
friend, a real friend, to another woman is a gift to both
of us.

Let's not take care of each other, however, even though
that's the plea on occasion. Being a friend doesn't mean
doing for someone what she needs to do for herself. It
means simply being there to listen, to love, to offer suggestions, to pray. In the end, we all have to be in charge
of ourselves. Being good role models for one another is a
genuine advantage of this program.

I will be a friend today and share myself,
my love, and my prayers with others.
I need friends too. They will be there for me.

If what we are doing with our anger is not achieving the desired result, it would seem logical to try something different.
—Harriet Lerner

How productive is anger? There is more than one school of thought. Some say we addicts can't afford to be angry. Others warn against repressing it. Learning simply to recognize anger is a big step for many of us. One thing we all agree on is that anger is a powerful feeling that affects us in many ways. If it goes unacknowledged, our relationships with others are damaged.

Anger is uncomfortable for many of us. We feel it often enough, but it makes us nervous anyway. Frequently we think we must be doing something wrong or we wouldn't be angry. Sometimes that's true. However, anger always signals that it's time to assess what we are projecting onto the situations or the people in our midst. Anger doesn't just happen. It's sown and cultivated by us.

If I get angry today I will look for the reason within myself. I can't change others, but I can change myself.

It is never the circumstances, but only your thoughts about them, that create your state of mind.
—Jane Nelsen

We all have at least one friend who seems unruffled by the unpredictable and changing circumstances of her life. How does she do it? People like her seem to trust that God is in charge and all things are happening for our ultimate good. While we scurry around, fretting and controlling as much as we can—usually to no avail—she stays quiet and feels blessed by her life.

The difference between her and us is the frantic activity that consumes our minds. We tend to react continuously to the events around us. Until now, observing events rather than reacting to them was never an option. But taking charge of our lives in this fashion releases our anxiety and fills us with peace. With time and practice we'll experience the serenity that our friend feels.

I have control of my thoughts. Nothing can upset me today unless I choose to let it.

JULY

It is now clear to me that from the beginning some human beings saw that the best way of taking life was lightly.
—Florida Scott-Maxwell

Not overreacting to the events in our lives is a major achievement for some of us. Thinking before acting is a learned behavior; we have time and many daily opportunities to learn it.

The people who seem to laugh easily, who are always ready with encouragement, who seldom are in a personal crisis, are obvious targets of our envy. What makes them different? Why don't they struggle like we do? It isn't fair, we think.

There's just one difference between them and us: it's called faith. They have it, and we can too. Beginning each day reflecting on the Serenity Prayer will help us develop the faith we lack. Giving to God the many problems we needlessly worry over lightens our load. Laughter can come more easily to us too.

Letting God handle my problems today will allow me more time to laugh.

Too many things in today's rushed and hurried world seem to require immediate action. I need to differentiate between the things that require immediate action and the things that can wait.
—Karen Davis

Not to get caught up in the flurry of activity around us takes monumental effort. It seems that everyone else is on a fast track, and if we abstain from the race, we worry about getting left behind, thus missing an opportunity that may surface only once in our lives.

In spite of our fears, very few circumstances need immediate attention. By taking the time to think through our alternatives and then to ask our Higher Power for guidance, we are assured the right response to every circumstance. With practice we will learn that pausing a moment or two won't mean missing an opportunity that has our name on it.

Some situations, such as a swerving car or an injured friend, require a quick response. However, even those circumstances call for reaction that is thoughtful rather than rushed. Every decision we make will be better when we let God give us a hand.

I can slow my pace today. My friends and I will benefit from my thoughtful responses.

In seeking a balanced life, I find so many excit-
ing opportunities to explore and understand that
none of them needs to become a compulsion.
—Michele Fedderly

Many of us long to live more balanced lives. We have been "all-or-nothing" women, and living on the edge may have excited us. Overcommitment to causes, people, or a social life kept us from thinking about ourselves. Then we'd crash, only to gather our resources to begin the frantic pace again. Our compulsive activity was countered by total retreat, again and again. The thread that remained the same was our reliance on some substance to take away the pain.

Are we free of pain now? Not always, but we have more positive ways to handle it. We have friends who will listen. We have sponsors who can suggest new ways to deal with our stumbling blocks. We know people who are living more balanced lives, and we can model ourselves after them. Now we have a reason for slowing down. We have come to believe that the present moment is all we really have.

Balancing my activities today will allow me
to accomplish more of what really needs to be done.

utting your emotional well-being in the hands of someone else is like riding a roller coaster into infinity.

—*Anonymous*

Giving someone else the power to make us sad or happy, angry or hopeful, confident or insecure is never beneficial. Taking charge of how we feel guarantees us as much happiness as we desire. This surprises many of us. Why didn't we know it before?

Codependency is common among women, particularly those of us who have addictions. Our search for security has endangered us more than once. We have followed others down dangerous paths when we thought love was the reward. We have denied our common sense when seeking the approval of others. We have put our values aside for a moment of acceptance. However, each moment is a chance for a new decision about who is in charge of how we feel. We can begin now to make a difference in our lives.

*I may not be happy today, but no one else
has the power to decide that for me
unless I give someone that power.*

My name is Elizabeth. I have a gift. It is called
alcoholism.
                                        —*Elizabeth Farrell*

Many of us didn't feel alcoholism or addiction was a gift when we first got into recovery. We felt shame or perhaps anger that we couldn't drink or use like other women. Alcohol or other drugs made us feel less self-conscious and more courageous. Accepting that we couldn't handle these substances meant feeling the fear of many situations, perhaps for the first time.

But most of us have come to appreciate the rewards of sobriety. When we were using, our lack of consistent values caused us to stumble many times. Now we have the Steps as guiding principles for every action we take.

We also have warm friendships that are healing our loneliness. We no longer harbor anger and self-pity. We are more peaceful and secure. Having a Higher Power we can trust makes any new experience tolerable. Addiction and sobriety are both gifts we have been graced with, and we are coming to appreciate this more each day.

I will show God my appreciation for the gifts
of addiction and sobriety by carrying
the message through my behavior today.

I always thought some people were just born with self-esteem and others not. The fact is, the people with self-esteem may have learned to develop it sooner than others, and now it's my turn.

—Laurel Lewis

One element of our growth is making new choices for ourselves. One of our choices is to have the self-esteem that is our right as a human being.

Some women may have never struggled with low self-esteem. Certainly, many women were born into families where unconditional love helped to develop the kind of self-esteem we crave. Yet with the help of this program and our Higher Power, we too will begin to feel a full measure of self-esteem.

Having self-esteem is really nothing more than beginning to understand and then accepting our worthiness in this vast panorama called life. We have always mattered to God and our fellow travelers, or we wouldn't be here. It's our beliefs that need to change—nothing more. We are worthy and loved children of God.

Self-esteem does not have to elude me today. My worth is guaranteed. God doesn't make junk!

I like to think my purpose in life is to love.
—Jane Nakken

Most would agree that we are *here* for a reason. Reflecting on where we have come from and the changes that have occurred in our lives, we are convinced that some Power has been present every step of the way. We do have both a purpose and a protector.

The panic to determine our specific purpose is not unusual for addicts like us. We demand absolutes; guesswork frightens us. But finding a sponsor who will tell us that our purpose doesn't matter will be to our benefit. From her we'll learn to take our experiences in stride, trusting that we'll discover who we are and what we need to do next if we accept life as it unfolds.

If we must have a purpose now, choosing to believe our purpose is loving others eases our way. And really, there is no purpose more worthy anyway.

Today I will express to others the love
I know my Higher Power has for me.
It's the best action I can take.

*No one can become a winner without losing
many, many times.*

—*Marie Lindquist*

The emphasis our society places on winning—whether it's a golf tournament, a relationship, or a promotion at work—heightens our shame of losing. And unfortunately, we define ourselves as losers all too easily.

It isn't possible to excel in every pursuit. Because we compare ourselves with others—this woman who plays tennis like a pro or that woman who just received a promotion—we give ourselves a failing grade. But do we ever look at another woman as a whole? She is just like us, really. Her successes are sprinkled among her many tries that miss their mark.

It takes perseverance to succeed at anything. Perhaps it's time to redefine success for ourselves and consider just making an attempt to do something well as success. It is, after all.

*As long as I try my best at relationships, work,
or play today, I will feel good about my efforts.*

I've become stronger and more positive as I've experienced life.
—JoAnn Reed

With the help of the program, we grow through our fears while we mature. As little girls, many things may have scared us—and for some of us, with good reason. The abuse or dysfunction we may have lived through made us wary of many people and situations.

We can't change the past. Whatever we experienced must be reckoned with. But we can believe that this program, the Twelve Steps, and the women who share our journey can help us accept the past, forgive the injustices, and become willing to believe in the possibility of a good life.

Because we're still here, we undoubtedly have a purpose to fulfill. We can learn what our special purpose is by opening ourselves to the messages we get from our trusted friends and from God in prayer. In time we'll perhaps see that the experiences we had as children give us special insights as adults. We are unfolding through the grace of God.

Today I will not be fear-filled. I am strong.
My friends, God, and this program
give me all the strength I need.

Asking God for help has finally become a part of my life. Now I'm learning to quiet myself to hear God's response.

—Joan Rohde

No problem is too insignificant for us to look to God for guidance. And every problem gives us an opportunity to strengthen our spiritual development. As we rely more on God for our sense of direction, we will encounter fewer situations that cause us turmoil. Trusting God's presence and guidance lessens the confusion that in past years may have crippled us.

Most of us came into this program with little or no belief in a loving Higher Power. It may have taken frequent suggestions from sponsors and other people in recovery for us to be willing to ask for the help we were promised. But finally we cleared that hurdle. Immediately we faced another one. Asking for help, we found, was the easier part; listening for God's reply was harder.

But the right reply will come to us at the right time. We will sense the answer we're looking for when the time for knowing it is right.

I will include my Higher Power in all my problem solving today. The solution I need will be mine if I patiently wait for the response.

We all get to choose how we perceive things.
—Chris DeMetsenaere

How happy do we really want to be? That's perhaps the most important question we can ask ourselves every morning. We are absolutely in charge of how we answer the question and how we feel all day long. What we forget, all too often, is that our thinking doesn't just happen to us. We create it. We are in charge of it. We are powerless over much, but our thoughts are our responsibility.

It's exhilarating to understand deeply the breadth of our power to perceive and feel. It became habitual for us to blame others for everything that happened to us and for our resulting feelings. Entrenched habits are hard to break, but it's an adventure and a rewarding challenge to develop healthier habits.

There is no better time than now to decide what kind of day we want and to create it!

*I will quietly and carefully choose how I see my
life today. I will feel as happy as I want to.*

One step at a time may seem too slow some days.
—Kay Marie Porterfield

Impatience is certainly not a virtue. However, we frequently display it as though it were: if we don't get some task done right now, we will have failed for all time. How many backfired circumstances must we have before we get the message?

When we came into this recovery program, we may have heard that there would always be enough time to accomplish what God intends us to do. Those of us who looked back at failed attempts doubted the truth of this wisdom. But we are coming to believe it now. In time, all the simple messages seem to come true.

The slogans are excellent examples of this. "One day at a time, one step at a time" will never fail us. We will handle whatever comes to us if we follow that advice.

I will accomplish what I need to today, on time,
if I let my Higher Power be in charge.

Thank God my future isn't what it used to be.
—*Jill Clark*

Most of us were on our way to an awful destination, and it's doubtful that we realized it at the time. In fact, we probably were satisfied with the direction we'd headed in and fiercely fought the forces that moved us off our chosen path. Fortunately, we lost the battle. In the process we gained this life, but it has taken time for us to understand how lucky we are to have been "saved."

God's grace has blessed us. We can call it "luck" or "karma" or "good planning" or an "accident," but we hear those in recovery calling it "grace." We know that they are right. Something intervened and changed the course of our lives.

We may not yet know just what our new direction is, but we can be certain that if we listen to the still, small voice within, we'll understand the meaning of the grace that's been bestowed on us.

My future is special. Today I'll be shown what I need to know for living the next twenty-four hours.

Before a geographical change can improve your life, you need to leave old thoughts and habits behind or you'll have the same problems in a new town.
—Anne Marie Nelson

We can't escape ourselves. Who we are tags along wherever we go. A spiteful attitude follows us to a new location. Self-pity doesn't leave us just because we change jobs. And our expectation of failure won't die just because we end a relationship. However, we can change our attitude, we can free ourselves of self-pity, and we can expect success when we take charge of who we are. Changing our external world can't do it. Changing our internal world guarantees it.

But aren't we simply *who we are?* How many times have we said, or heard others say, "That's just who I am," as though all hope of being different is out of the question? While it is true that we are who we are, who we want to be is always in our control. We have the power to change any aspect of our character.

My old habits have been discarded.
I have no reason to pick them up today.
The new me is here.

My few close, lasting friends are precious to me.
We seem to help center each other as our lives
travel parallel paths.
                                                —Robyn Halsema

We are walking in concert with many other people. It is not an accident that we have been drawn into the lives of the people who surround us. Our destinies are entwined. We have the opportunity to learn from one another, to help one another, and to grow in our trust that there are no accidents in this God-filled world.

Some days we may fear the circumstances edging toward us. We may doubt that the people involved have our best interests at heart. At those times we need to look to our precious relationships for strength and courage. Just as our friends are with us by design, so are the circumstances from which we will learn our much-needed lessons.

We are never alone. Our friends are only a call away. Our Higher Power is at our service. The love surrounding us centers us and makes us whole and strong and serene.

I rejoice in the knowledge that my loved ones
are here by design. My fears will diminish when
I am in the company of my friends and God.

Filling the hole in our soul with contemplation, meditation, and prayer will teach us that the God of our understanding is there.
—Jan Lloyd

We are coming to understand that our Higher Power has always been present. That's why we survived our addiction. However, cultivating a friendship with this unseen presence takes willingness and discipline. It helps if we converse with this God of our understanding every day. This friendship is much like all our other friendships in that it can be strengthened by attention.

The more time we give to God, the more smoothly our lives will unfold. When we learn to make no decision without first consulting God, we will dramatically change the outcome of many of our experiences. Even while in the midst of a trying situation, we can seek God's guidance and be freed from unnecessary harm.

In the past we desperately tried to fill the void with alcohol or other drugs; now we're filling it with love for our Higher Power. How lucky we are that we have lots of living yet to do.

My experiences today will reflect my closeness to the God I trust. Remembering this assures me of a peaceful day.

I have to remember to tell the negative committee
that meets in my head to sit down and shut up.
—Kathy Kendall

Why does it seem easier to get trapped in negative thinking than it does to have positive expectations? Maybe it's
only a matter of habit. We may be proficient at expecting
the worst outcomes, but with the support and the example of friends who share our journey today, we can break
that habit. And we'll discover that it's not that difficult.

Let's begin by making small attempts. In the past our
mind seemed to fill up with random thoughts, as if it were
a news show produced by an outsider. Today, as quick as
a blink, we can fast-forward the picture to one we prefer.
We can be the full-time producer of our own news show.
That's the good news!

Our thoughts and attitudes are there by our choice. We
must acknowledge that. We can neither blame nor give
credit to anyone but ourselves. We can make a habit of
positive thinking. Let's begin right now.

I will focus on positive thoughts today.
Remembering that my thoughts are
of my own making, every time,
makes it easier to switch channels.

*Life is so much easier if you ride the horse in the
direction it's going.*
                                        —*Anonymous*

There is a pattern to our lives. Our Higher Power has
always wanted the best for us. Had we trusted the natural flow of our experiences instead of trying to control
people and outcomes, we'd have experienced less pain
and lots more joy. It's not that life won't have difficult
lessons to teach us on occasion. It will, and they may
hurt. But we must remember that God will never give us
what we can't handle and, furthermore, that we'll have
the guidance we need to meet our challenges.

Going against our inner urges never gives us peace.
The wisdom that resides within is a gift from our Higher
Power. Let's never forget that.

*I will be peaceful today if I follow
the voice of my heart.*

I do not have to always be right!
—Mary Zink

Where does the need to be right come from? No doubt from our youth and the shaming reprimands that were heaped on us by parents and teachers when we made mistakes. We mastered the idea that we weren't worthy unless we knew everything and lived mistake-free lives. Of course this was impossible; thus, we felt like failures most of the time. That is, until we discovered this program.

We are free at last. Free from the torment of trying to be perfect. Free from the torment of trying to know everything. Free from the torment of trying to control others against their will. Free from the agitation that came all too easily even in minor disagreements. We feel as if we have been born anew, and we have, more or less.

We are right part of the time, but the burden of having to be right in order to *be at all* is gone. And that has made all the difference.

I will be right part of the time today.
I'll let others be right their fair share too.

*If I want to feel better, I need to tell someone how
I feel. If a friend in recovery asks me how I am,
I answer honestly. Something special occurs. We
are kindred spirits.*
—Marianne Lunde

We have a choice. We can isolate ourselves with our
problems and remain stuck in their pain, or we can
share with a friend or a sponsor what's troubling us and
as a result experience serenity.

When we were using, we withdrew from the world,
hiding the thoughts and feelings that haunted us.
Dwelling in the scary places all alone, we felt even more
distant and alienated from the very people who might
have helped us discover some peace.

At last those days are over. We are on this journey
together, and we will help one another find the joy we
deserve. We have only two assignments today or any day:
one is to share honestly, openly, and lovingly with someone else who we really are; the other is to listen with a
caring heart as another woman shares her story. Both of
us will discover a peacefulness that neither of us has felt
before.

*It is my choice today whether to stay isolated and sick,
or to reach out and help two people: me and a sister
in need. Help me, God, to want to help my sister.*

A quiet mind is one of the best cures for a low mood.

—Jane Nelson

It may seem too simple that we can change a bad mood or a bad attitude by "getting quiet." But in fact, we can. Clearing our thoughts of anger, resentment, self-pity, and fear gives us the space to feel peaceful. And within these spaces we discover, again, our gratitude.

Each of us has countless things for which to feel grateful, but acknowledging this is hard when we are low. Let's do it together: We have this program to help us handle whatever comes, one day at a time. We have as many friends as we want; all we have to do is go to meetings. We have a sponsor who cares; her help is never more than a phone call away. A Higher Power intervened in our lives, or we wouldn't be here. We have come to believe a Higher Power will be with us always.

Gratitude is a decision. It comes naturally when we quiet our minds of the negative noise.

If I feel low today, I have some tools to use. Letting go of the thoughts that harm me is the first one to try.

*We need to make a distinction between power-
lessness and owning our power.*

—Melody Beattie

We are powerful women. But we may have misused our
power at times. We may have tried for years to wield
control over others. Unfortunately, it took too many
conflicts for us to accept that we didn't have almighty
power over others. On the other hand, being powerless
over others doesn't mean being victims. Owning our
personal power is healthy. There's much that we can
be responsible for. Today is a good day to focus on this.
For example, we have the power to smile at everyone we
meet. We can control the words we speak on every occasion. We can choose to harbor positive thoughts.

We have the power to accept all experiences as lessons.
Most important, we have the power to pursue whatever
brings pleasure to our lives.

*I am not powerless over what I do, think,
or say today. I have all the power I need
to have whatever kind of day I want.*

When I lean on a door and it collapses, it cannot all be attributed to my strength; something must be said for the infirm condition of the door. This keeps my ego in check.

—Ruth Humlecker

We love to take credit for God's work. Because our will is consistent with God's on occasion, we fool ourselves into thinking we control events and people. Unfortunately, when we try to force conditions to suit our plans, we frequently trample on the spirit of others.

We are too invested in being right. When we are not right—which is often—we are certain others measure us as unworthy. Our self-absorption tells us that others see us through our eyes. In reality, others seldom take notice of our failings. We win some battles. We successfully orchestrate some experiences. God's outcomes match our desires when appropriate. But we aren't the power behind the successes; we are only the instrument.

*I am not the cause of someone's success
or failure today. I may help God's plan,
but I can't make it happen.*

Yes, I made up my mind . . .
today I do have a choice,
and I like the idea of
being a smiling Goddess.
                        —Betty MacDonald

Many of us grew up either afraid of making choices or unaware that multiple options were open to us. Until we get accustomed to the idea of deciding for ourselves what to do first, where to live, what to believe, we are overwhelmed with the possibilities. Yet in recovery, we are thrilled with the knowledge that we are re-creating ourselves. Recovery has given us this gift. Our continued sobriety means we can keep it.

Giving to others the love we now know honors the Goddess within. Choosing to share love with others gives us greater awareness of our inner Goddess every day.

I will make the choice to love others today.
The more love I give away, the more love I'll feel.

Dare to be empty.
Dare to let go.
Dare to believe.
—*Elisabeth L.*

We seldom receive a direct, visual experience of God. Most of us only sense a Presence, or perhaps see the evidence of God's help. It takes profound faith to live moment by moment in the knowledge that God is always here.

The founders of AA understood how difficult it is to believe. The tools of this program can help us with our struggle. In using them, we let God guide us, protect us, comfort us, and take charge of everyone else too. Asking sponsors for examples of how they have let go will help us see our opportunities more clearly. Coupling their suggestions and experiences with practice at using the Steps and slogans will strengthen our willingness to turn to God for everything.

I will be able to let God take charge if I rely
on the example and experience of the friends
I know I can trust. Today can be easy.

We are social beings not from habit, and not for
convenience or expediency, but of necessity.
—Mary McDermott Shideler

What does it really mean that we need each other?
Being strong and independent were qualities we strove
for. Most of us were encouraged to learn how to stand
on our own two feet. Doesn't that advice fly in the face
of needing others?

The truth is, we have lessons to learn and contributions
to make. Our relationships with others provide us with
those opportunities. None of us are here without reason.
Our lives are blended for a much greater purpose than
what our narrow, individual focus sees. The group, the
community that claims our membership, has been assem-
bled by God. Let's know that we need to be here, now.

I need the people who surround me now.
I may not understand the reason, but I don't need to.
Trust is all that's necessary.

*To not accept all of ourselves creates polarity. Try
to live your life only inhaling for five minutes.*
—Niro Asistent

Not all of our qualities are admirable. In fact, some embarrass us. There is nothing preventing us from developing more positive characteristics, but the inspiration to do so often wanes. It might be more reasonable to strengthen the good ones with more frequent use and learn to love the rest as evidence of our very human nature.

We are complex personalities. We have been years in development, and we aren't finished yet. Each day gives us opportunities to demonstrate a whole range of qualities.

We can accept each personal trait. That doesn't mean we have to love every aspect of what we say or do. Nor does it mean we should never try to change. But taking our life, our behavior, more in stride will give us the heart to change what we can.

*I am both good and bad. If I want to accentuate
my positive traits, it is up to me to practice them today.*

*Keeping hearts happy is a lot like keeping bodies
healthy. We need to feed our hearts well through
reading, prayer, and meditation, and to exercise
them by loving.*
                                              —Jane Nakken

Our well-being is the result of concentrated effort. While
we may know people who seem to be secure, happy, and
serene all the time, we are seldom privy to all the work
they have put into this attitude. Spiritual exercise pays
off. Those we admire are examples of it.

Each of us can be an example of it too. Taking some time
alone with our Higher Power every day is a good way to
begin our exercise. Developing a trusting friendship with
God guarantees us the guidance we long for throughout
our lives. Coming to believe that God is always present,
we can respond to all our experiences with peaceful and
loving hearts. We won't live in fear of people or events
when we have exercised our trust in and reliance on God.

*I will exercise some effort today to connect
with my Higher Power. My efforts
will affect all my experiences.*

Every once in a while I make a list of my obses-
sions. Some obsessions change and there are
always more. Some are thankfully forgotten.
—Natalie Goldberg

It's not just the disease of addiction that causes ob-sessions; some say that being human is all it takes. Obsessions are generally triggered by wanting some-thing or somebody to change. The problem is that al-though we don't have the power to change other people, we dwell incessantly on the possibility.

Through the help of the Twelve Steps, we are gradually becoming aware that we can change no one but ourselves. That doesn't mean we'll immediately quit obsessing about what others should do, but we now have the tools to rec-ognize what is in our control and what isn't. We can get rid of obsessions.

My obsession with anything today means I have
forgotten what is in my control and which
tools can help me. I'll look to a friend for guidance.

We alone cannot heal the betrayals in our lives, but our inner spirit's healing power can enter our souls and soothe our pain with understanding, acceptance, and love.

—Rita Casey

Betrayal is a reality of our lives. Perhaps a parent or a spouse was the perpetrator. No one of us escaped it. And just as we were betrayed, we quite likely were betrayers too. We are not perfect human beings. We did the best we could with what we knew.

Now we know so much more. Had our betrayers had the information we now cherish, they'd likely have been quite different. Fortunately, we can look to our Higher Power (our Inner Spirit) to ease the pain that still lingers. With the strength of this spirit and our willingness to forgive our betrayers, we can find peace and feel love once again. What we know now convinces us that a forgiving heart heals.

I will reap wonderful rewards today if I let my Inner Spirit help me to forgive.

*Turn a disadvantage into an advantage; embrace
that which is unfair.*
—Eileen Fehlen

We have all heard the saying "When life gives you
lemons, make lemonade." We may have been certain at
times that a particular batch of lemons was far too sour
to be redeemed. But we do not know what lesson might
be in store for us in a particular set of circumstances. We
can be certain only that God is in charge of the lesson
and the outcome. Our part is to stay positive and hopeful, and to trust, to turn our life and our will over to
God.

Embracing that which seems unfair is merely showing
our loving Higher Power that we trust the ebb and flow of
our lives. It doesn't mean that we love what is happening;
instead, it means that we are willing to let go and let God
direct our actions. Though letting go may be difficult at
first, when we grow accustomed to it, we will feel a great
burden lifted from our shoulders. Giving our life to God
to manage means giving ourselves freedom to laugh and
play more. We deserve the relief. We deserve the joy this
guarantees. And we will find it!

*I deserve a peaceful, joy-filled life.
If I let God help me today, I will feel so much better.*

AUGUST

*Let us not become involved in terminal
seriousness.*
—Julie Riebe

Developing a healthy and balanced perspective is one of
the gifts of this program. However, we have to work at
it. It doesn't happen by simply laying the alcohol or other
drugs aside. We need the help of caring sponsors who
say "So what!" when we get on the pity pot. We also need
the help of our Higher Power.

We soon discover that the more involved we get with
the Steps of this program and the more we let God take
an active role in our lives, the easier all situations become.
We also discover that letting God play a part doesn't
mean that we no longer have a responsible part to play;
instead, it means that we no longer are trying to take full
responsibility for the outcome of every experience that
engages us. Gaining this healthy perspective on our lives
is a profound blessing. Were it not for this program and
all the help we are receiving, we'd still be manufacturing
mountains from every molehill, or molehills from every
mountain.

*I will utilize the program and my Higher Power today
to keep situations in their proper perspective.*

God can work quicker in our lives if God doesn't
have to seek out our hiding place.
　　　　　　　　　　　　　　　　—Jan Pishok

What do we gain from wallowing in doubt and hiding from God? Certainly not peace or security. But the pain is familiar. We often hang on to that which we know, regardless of its impact.

In the past, many of us had an attitude, and we nurtured a chip on our shoulder. What a relief to be free of that childish burden! Hiding from God means missing the real gifts of sobriety. Putting alcohol or other drugs aside, but not grasping the hand of God as it comes to us from our friends, means the torment that triggered our drinking and using continues to follow close on our heels.

We are learning from our sisters sharing this journey that there's a far less traumatic way to live. Our assignment is simply to turn to God every day, letting our will and lives be thus guided.

I won't hide today. I'll seek God in all
my communications with others,
and I'll cherish the peace.

Life does not accommodate you, it shatters you. . . .
Every seed destroys its container or else there
would be no fruition.
—Florida Scott-Maxwell

We resist change because it shatters our self-perceptions. But if we don't change, our journey's purpose is stunted. As we look back, we can see that change is a constant among our experiences. But we often resist it until the pain is more than we can bear.

It's curious that we'd expect our lives to stay the same despite what we see: movement, new growth, change. Year by year we note the deeper lines and the lesser energy in our parents, our siblings, ourselves. The trees shed their leaves, the sidewalk cracks widen, the neighbors move away. Change happens. Our purpose will be fulfilled.

Being grateful for change comes only with willingness and the trust that we deserve growth and opportunity. What's in store for each of us is far greater than what we can imagine for ourselves.

I might not like everything that happens today,
but each experience will offer me
an opportunity to change.

Retreat is not defeat!
—Kay Lovatt

Sometimes the most productive thing we can do is back away from a situation that's causing us pain. Every time we feel compelled to resolve a crisis, we can retreat, at least for a time. Giving our emotions a rest gives us a fresh perspective.

Trying to force another person to see a situation as we do seldom works, just as we can't be convinced against our will that someone else is right. The history we carry colors our view. But we can learn from one another; that's why we are sharing this journey.

Does it seem that we encourage conflicts? Is our security tied to having others validate our opinions? Perhaps turning to our Higher Power each time we anticipate conflict will relieve us of the need to express an opinion that's not crucial to the moment.

I don't have to resolve anything today.
I can simply go along with how things are
and trust that they will change, with God's help.

If one lives, one experiences betrayal.
—Ruth Casey

Betrayal is a hateful action. We have all experienced betrayal, sometimes even from those we love. The pain is seldom forgotten. Unfortunately, betraying others is a human failing we all share. Each of us wants to be counted on, and we intend to live up to the expectations we have of ourselves. We sometimes falter, however, and hurt others by our actions. Pain is the result, every time, whether we betray another or are betrayed.

Perhaps our best hope for avoiding betrayal is relying on the Third Step for guidance before taking action. Stopping a moment to reflect before taking any action can change the tenor of every situation.

I have experienced betrayal. Even worse,
I have betrayed others. Today will be different.
I will listen to my Higher Power.

As we cultivate stillness and commune with the
Presence within, we are mightily enhanced.
                                    —*Marsha Sinetar*

When we retreat to our quiet interior spaces, we grow
in our understanding of God and life's mysteries. The
richness we come to know through keeping our spiritual
life simple is unexpected.

Spiritual leaders from all faiths have suggested we go
within to know God and, thus, ourselves. The founders
of our program suggested likewise. It was their hope that
we might find the peace and freedom that only God can
guarantee. The Steps are our tools for knowing God.

Each day that we rely on our spiritual connection to
clarify our direction, we'll discover the serenity that
enhances our being. Perhaps we didn't need our addictions to know God, but they are serving as the pathway
to our freedom.

I consider myself lucky to be an alcoholic
or addict. It has given me a connection
to God that is enriching my life.

I used to think, this is just the way I am. Now I know that I create myself anew—every day.
                                                              —Jill Clark

Even when we wallowed in drugs and self-pity, we were in charge of our choices. Try as we might to blame others for our failures, the buck stops here.

The necessity of taking responsibility for our entire life may be one of the hardest lessons we have to learn. We can start accepting responsibility by following the example of others in this circle of recovery. We can quit blaming parents, teachers, siblings, or neighbors for our problems and habitual defects of character.

We must finally accept that we always had choices on how to respond to every transgression against us. As youngsters we may not have felt empowered to stand up for ourselves, but we must take that step now or be forever stuck in the patterns of the past.

Today is a clean slate. I will be me,
whoever I decide "me" is.
I will become a work of art today.

*Most of us spend our energy seeking the highs in
an effort to avoid the lows. Unfortunately, these
false highs are not really nourishing.*

—Niro Asistent

Emotional highs energize us. All of us experience them.
Most of us crave them, but unfortunately they are short-
lived. When external circumstances elevate our mood,
their absence brings us back down. Highs like these set
us up for disappointment.

Recovery can change this aspect of our lives. Using the
Twelve Steps, we are able to experience highs as a natural response to our interior activity. Feeling as good as we
want to feel, every day, is possible when we decide to use
the Steps: to look to our Higher Power for knowledge of
what to do on a daily basis, to seek comfort when we are
filled with fear, to receive courage when amends are in
order. Our emotions will reflect how consistently we use
the Steps. We can be energized by highs every day if we
so desire.

*I can feel a nourishing high today if I use
the tools of the program to guide me.*

God loves us so much that whatever fills our minds is what God thinks we want.
—Dudley Martineau

What do we commonly dwell on? For some of us, it's how we fail to measure up to our expectations. Exaggerating and dwelling on our imperfections keep us stuck.

Sponsors tell us that God gives us what we think we want, but how does that work? Does whatever we hold in our mind become real? Carefully reviewing what has happened may convince us of this. Many experiences we dreaded indeed materialized. Just as often, fantasies we seldom dared to dream didn't come our way.

While it's true that there is much over which we have no control, the thoughts we dwell on are within our power. Every thought we harbor is a direct communication to God. We will experience what we keep asking for through the thoughts we send to God.

God is listening to every thought I have today. I will get what I want.

Life is short; eat dessert first.
                                    —*Joy Sommers*

Some say that attitude is everything. Many of us have endured abusive families, unreasonable bosses, and the uncertainty of illness. But not all of us carry the pain and fear of the past into the present. We have found new patterns of thinking and behaving now that we've come to this program for help. Here we cultivate the attitude that we each are doing the best we can with the knowledge we have. We can forgive ourselves for our transgressions.

When we decide to let go of experiences that can't be changed, we find so much more joy in the present. The decision to seek joy and love now is like eating dessert first. The quickening pace of our lives as we age is reason enough to grasp every moment and savor its joy.

Being more light-hearted today promises
me memories worth savoring.

*It is as blessed to receive as it is to give and a
lot harder.*
—Ruth Humlecker

We think we are unworthy. Compliments on our appearance, praise for our work, strokes for our efforts to help others often go unappreciated by us. Why can't we hear them? Why don't we take them in? No doubt it's because of shame for not being perfect. None of us are perfect, but all of us think that perfection is possible and we have failed the test. How futile the thought. How harmful the result.

We are adept at many things; we are perfect at none. That's a fact of human life. But we are good enough, providing we do our best and rely on God for direction. Coming to believe this is perhaps our most important lesson in life.

*If someone blesses me with a compliment today,
I will quietly listen and believe it is true.*

A big part of my "conversion" has been full acceptance of myself, warts and all.

—Mary Zink

Every day is a fresh opportunity to love ourselves a little bit more and judge ourselves a little bit less. Growing up with overly critical parents, as many of us did, has made it hard to believe we're okay. But here, in a Twelve Step program, we receive the affirmation we deserve on a daily basis.

We are never going to be perfect. We can't even define what that means. Perhaps God is perfect. Elements of nature appear perfect. But we humans are flawed. And yet we are all okay just as we are. Certainly, we can improve our condition. Doing an inventory will reveal the substantive changes we might make in ourselves. It's good to remember, however, that we are loved unconditionally by our Higher Power and our friends. Learning to accept and appreciate who we are is the most productive lesson we'll ever learn.

I am worthy and lovable.
My belief will grow with practice.

Laughter, like a drenching rain, settles the dust, cleans and brightens the world around us, and changes our whole perspective.
—Jan Pishok

Laughter's power is awesome. Some might say miraculous. We all know the effects of laughter. Even in the midst of frustrating circumstances, nothing seems as bleak or hopeless after being observed through the twinkling eyes of laughter.

How is it that our perspective changes after a moment or two of laughter? Does laughing shake loose the cobwebs that clutch the grim realities? All we know for certain is that nothing appears quite the same after we switch our focus from the dark to the light.

Laughter refreshes us. We can't change the people we love, we can't determine outcomes, we can't control how God works in our lives. But we can laugh. And laughing about our experiences gives us the chance to accept them and make them work to our advantage.

Nothing is quite as serious as I make it today.
Lightening up and laughing a little
makes every minute easier.

*Life is perfect, just the way it is and just the way
it is not.*

—*Peggy Bassett*

Coming to believe that life is perfect however it is takes
willingness and concentrated faith. Most of us waste
precious hours every day wishing for something that
isn't. Will we ever learn?

It isn't wrong to want some things to be different. If
our own behavior can inspire positive changes in ourselves or others, then it's not wrong to take responsibility
for what we can do. What is futile, though, is assuming
we know what is best for everyone. We can't see the big
picture. God gives us only what we need right now. What
may look like trouble, what may appear as imperfect one
minute, may be God's greater plan. Let's wait and see.

*I will find comfort in the message that all is well.
I will use that today if I get worried
about how events seem to be unfolding.*

*I have discovered that while God would do for me
what I could not do for myself, God would not do
for me what I could do for myself.*
—Mary Norton Gordon

There are some things God is always in charge of. One is
outcomes. Another is the big picture encompassing our
lives. Each experience is part of God's design for us. On
occasion, we may feel there is little for us to do, since
God will handle it all. However, the truth is, our participation is necessary. Every day we have many opportunities to thoughtfully put one foot in front of the other.
How lovingly, how gently, how honestly and openly we
move through our lives—all these things color the experiences God has planned for us.

We may sometimes find ourselves sitting back, waiting
for God to take charge, or aggressively trying to force an
outcome that belongs only to God. But we are learning.
With time in the program, we begin to realize what is
God's work and what is ours. Our sponsors, the women
who share their experiences in meetings, prayer, and
meditation enlighten us about how it works.

*I am surrounded by women who can help me
distinguish between my job and God's job today.
My confusion won't trouble me for long.*

*Life is a process of learning to unlearn untruths
someone else believes.*
—Laurel Lewis

The *truth* for each of us is unique. We may share values
and opinions on many matters, but our perception is colored by our personal history.

Many of us grew up in or still live in families that
demand our allegiance to beliefs we don't honestly share.
Pretending doesn't fit us anymore. Perhaps it never did,
but we lacked the strength to stand up for our beliefs. We
wanted desperately to fit in and be loved. We still do, but
we want to respect ourselves too. We can do that only
when we're true to what we believe, regardless of the
beliefs of our family members or friends.

At first it's painful to break away from the beliefs that
other people want us to share: we feel isolated and vulnerable. Let's look to the women who are striving to grow
in this same way to support us in our struggle. Knowing
they understand our fear to be "us" makes knowing our
personal truth all the more possible.

*I will agree with the beliefs of some on my path today
and disagree with others. I'll ask my Higher Power
for the courage to speak my own truth.*

Shut up and listen!
—Anne Arthur

Sometimes we need to do ourselves a favor and "shut up and listen." Depending on our family, we may have heard the words "Shut up!" many times daily. To counter the verbal abuse, we might have learned to carry on an inner dialogue to drown out these words. That way of coping served us well. However, it became our habit to shut others out, regardless of their words, and now we need to break that habit. It serves us no more. In fact, it harms us.

We have learned that our Higher Power often tries to reach us through the words of a friend. If we have an inner dialogue going on, we will not hear the guidance we seek. We have heard many times in Twelve Step meetings the saying "When the student is ready, the teacher appears." Being quiet is being ready.

I will be ready for my lesson today.
I will listen intently to the words of my friends.

I like to look at perfection as continual expansion.
It's only when I stagnate and am afraid of change
that I am imperfect.

—Carlotta Posz

Perfection is a coat of many colors. Some people think we are perfect just as we are, simply because we are children of God. Others think that perfection is an unattainable goal because we must release all shortcomings and strengthen all assets to attain it. From sponsors we learn that any effort to live more peace-filled lives heightens our sense of a more perfect existence.

Perfection, like beauty, is in the eye of the beholder. Luckily, we are surrounded by loving friends who can help us see our progress when we are blind to all but our failed attempts.

Our attempts to grow, learn, change, and love others more fully will satisfy our Higher Power completely. These acts, repeatedly made, will cultivate in us the only perfection that truly counts.

I will do the best I can today toward my
loved ones and all others I meet. If I do that,
God will view my actions as "perfect."

I am the sole author of the dictionary that
defines me.
                                        —*Zadie Smith*

The people around us influence what we believe. Sometimes that's okay, but what happens when we are with a group of friends who don't all think alike? What do we believe then?

Self-assessment, as suggested in the Fourth Step, helps us define ourselves. It helps us understand who we are and what we believe, separate from the others in our lives. We discover we are who we are! We aren't who our friends want us to be, unless, of course, that fits us.

Having values that we understand and feel comfortable with makes a difference in how we perceive ourselves in our relationships. We are empowered every time we speak from our own center.

I will share with others who I really am today.
My personal judgment in all matters
will be lovingly revealed.

There is no healing without forgiveness. I love the
peace I feel with forgiveness.
                                                    —Helen Casey

The program is helping us understand that when we feel resentful or angry, we are hindering our own recovery as well as our Higher Power's plan for us. We cannot receive God's full message if we are trapped by our hateful feelings.

Why would we want to continue our agitation toward someone else, particularly when it means we can feel no peace? The answer lies in our struggle to be "right" in every situation. Being right rather than peaceful remains too important to us. But observing women who are serene will enlighten us about the possibilities for change the program promises. These possibilities can be ours if we change our attitude, develop the willingness to let go of past hurts, and live in a forgiving present.

It may sound difficult to live in a forgiving present, but it's not. We make the decision and then ask God to help us. Our hearts will heal and our resentments will be gone. Peace can become our permanent companion.

Serenity is my goal today; forgiveness of others
is the way I can achieve my goal.

The deeper our roots, the farther from home we can safely travel.
— Molly McDonald

When we think of our roots, we think of our family of origin, our birthplace, our youth. Who we are today, how we think about our opportunities, how we handle stress and pain—all are colored by the experiences of our past. But we are taking several steps to develop new roots too.

Learning from one another in this program helps establish the new root system. Understanding God's role in our lives strengthens the root system. Adhering to the Steps and the principles of this program nourishes the root system. All three keep us grounded in the healthy, serene life we have chosen. These new roots will give us the strength we need to handle any situation. They will lighten our burdens. They will comfort us like the arms of a loving parent. They will make our steps certain and our vision hopeful.

Venturing away from our home, whether it's our home group or our place of residence, is easier when we acknowledge the importance of taking our new way of life with us.

*My life here today and in all my tomorrows
will give me as much joy as my heart can contain.*

In a storm, the tree that bends with the wind is the one that survives to grow tall.
—Brenda Schaeffer

Sometimes we don't pick our battles rationally. Resistance from anyone, about anything, can make us miss the splendor of the moment. There is another way to live. We may not have observed it often in our own families, but we can learn the pattern nonetheless. It's called nonresistance.

Nonresistance means we stop trying to make something happen in only one way—our way. Nonresistance is refreshing. Suddenly we have more energy for fun activities, and we discover our presence is sought more often by the people we care about.

Giving up trying to force situations and people to follow our life plan is like doubling the possibilities for our own life. What a gift letting the rest of the world alone proves to be.

I won't do battle with anyone today.
I am in charge of only myself.

Advice from others applies to them.
—Georgette Vickstrom

Those of us who share this program are learning how to care about others, and it is natural that we want to help one another. Of course, that means we may suggest, sometimes too strongly, what we think a friend ought to do. We are frequently on the receiving end of similar suggestions. We can be glad that others want to help. We suffered alone with our problems for far too long. However, no one's advice can exactly fit our situation. Nor can ours fit theirs. The perspective that guides each of us is unique to our experiences.

It is never wrong to offer our support. Nor is it wrong, if asked, to share what we would do if the problem were ours. But to say to anyone, "Here is what you should do," is harmful. Let God play God.

I will not give unwanted suggestions or advice
to anyone today. God is the best guide for each of us.

The subconscious can be programmed to procure
the results you desire.
                                        —Susan Smith Jones

The subconscious absorbs events in the external world
as well as our internal world. It's never at rest. Yet we do
have power over what we cultivate in the recesses of our
subconscious.

There are some tools we can use to weed out unhealthy
messages from our subconscious. One is to replace negative thoughts with thoughts that nurture us. Another is
to develop affirmations that boost our self-esteem, and to
practice saying them while in a meditative state or standing before a mirror. Maybe the most effective of all tools
is visualization. Do it this way: Carefully paint the por-
trait of the woman you want to be in your mind. See her
in myriad situations, always performing superbly. Dwell
on her strengths, her capabilities in every experience.
Believe in her and she will become real.

I am who I think I can be today. My imagination
will shape the person I desire to be. I am in charge.

When my heart is overflowing with gratitude,
there is no room for fear.
—Kathy Kendall

Feelings can consume us. Sometimes we have positive feelings; other times we have negative feelings. The truth is, we can't harbor opposing emotions at the same time. If we are fearful, we can't be joyful and enthusiastic about what lies ahead. Conversely, if we are joyful and enthusiastic, we can't be fearful about what lies ahead.

The good news is that our feelings don't control us. It's quite the opposite. While it may seem that feelings overcome us, the truth is, they follow our thoughts. In other words, what we manufacture in our minds gives rise to our feelings. That means, of course, that we don't have to harbor any feeling one minute longer than we choose.

Deciding to feel grateful is just as easy as it is to feel hurt or resentful or fearful. We may not have all we desire, but we do have multiple blessings, each one of us. The more we give thanks to this program and our Higher Power, the more our blessings will multiply.

I will feel at one with my Higher Power today.
I am safe, clean and sober, and in caring hands.
There is nothing to fear.

*Whatever the mind pictures and expects, that it
will also build and produce for you!*
—*Catherine Ponder*

Our addiction fed our belief that others were responsible
for how we acted. That has made it hard to accept that
we are in charge and have been all along. Our personal
power is nearly beyond comprehension. The images we
carry in our minds become our reality.

This program and its principles can guide our thoughts
and so give us hope that we can have more positive lives.
We can quiet our minds and deliberately decide what to
dwell on. We usher in the reality we deserve when we
picture joy and loving interactions with people, when we
create the positive details we long for in our relationships,
our jobs, our personal attitudes.

*I am in control of how I see and experience
my life today. My mind is always at work,
but I'm its boss!*

*We are not separate from everything else. It's only
our egos that make us think we are.*
— *Natalie Goldberg*

As we grow and change spiritually, we come to understand our necessary connections to others. But this
doesn't happen quickly for most of us. Commonly, we
saw others as competitors, and we eagerly or fearfully
sought to outrank them. We learn from the wiser ones
in this program that every person contributes to what
each of us must learn. This gives us fresh appreciation of
our many relationships. None of them is accidental. All
of them are divine.

The peace that comes with accepting everyone as valuable to our existence is both refreshing and awesome. The
haunting anxiety of a lifetime begins to wither, and we
dare to feel contented, hopeful, and finally joyful. What a
pleasant experience the rest of our lives will be, as long as
we remember this.

*I am a partner to everyone I meet today.
I will trust my Higher Power's choices for me.*

Spiritual experience is personal and individual.
—*Veronica Ray*

We envy people who have had profound spiritual experiences. In comparison, our experiences often look meager. But the tiny awarenesses we have that God has always been present in our lives are as convincing as the most awesome experiences. We simply need to recognize them as evidence.

When situations fail to please us or other people seem out of control, we long for our Higher Power to be more present in our lives. But we are slowly coming to understand that everyone else has a Higher Power; when others aren't living according to our will, perhaps they are living according to their God's will.

When we come to terms with God's role in our lives, we'll feel more assurance about our own role and be more aware of the myriad, concrete examples of the spiritual experiences we have had.

My experience with God is very much my own.
It does not resemble someone else's experience.
God considers my needs unique.

Willing to be oneself is not always easy, especially when . . . we are not at all sure who we are.
—*Mary McDermott Shideler*

It's normal to mimic the expressions and the opinions of the people we admire. We did it as girls. We continue to do it. Fortunately, our taste in friends and models has improved. We have now surrounded ourselves with women who are in recovery and who have chosen honest, spiritually focused lives.

A goal of our recovery is to discover and celebrate who we really are. It's time to focus on what we actually think, what we really feel, who we prefer being. This self-discovery is empowering, yet arduous and humbling. Because we are human and not perfect, we come face-to-face with traits that signal our need for growth. This journey into self-discovery changes us forever. We can never so easily mimic others again.

I can be the person I want to be today.
I now have the courage to choose my actions
rather than imitate someone else's.

I cannot have what I want if I do not wish it for others.
                                            —Betty MacDonald

Envy is familiar to many of us. We may spend far too much time comparing ourselves with others and grading ourselves as inadequate. Focusing on what others have never allows us to feel grateful for our blessings or generous in spirit. Paradoxically, what we want for others comes back to us.

This is a simple principle, but like other new ideas, we have to "wear it" for a while to get its meaning; we have to practice it faithfully to get its effect. Perhaps initially we can better see its reverse. Let's recall a few times when we have harbored mean thoughts toward another or wished ill will on an acquaintance. Our own spirit felt the repercussions. Maybe bad luck didn't overtly trip us, but we never feel good for long when we cultivate a mean-spirited attitude. Everyone is served by our good wishes. Let's work on that today.

If I catch myself feeling jealous or mean,
I'll take charge of my thoughts.
Only I can turn them around.

It took me years to get this way. I can't expect to change in just one day.
— *Jill Clark*

Now that we are sober, it's not unusual to expect everything to be perfect overnight. Placing unreasonable demands on ourselves is symptomatic of our disease. We are filled with shame for all the time we have wasted and all the people we have disappointed. We feel we must make up for all our transgressions at once so we can get on with our lives. But we can get on with life anyway. Simply deciding to change one thing is a significant step in the right direction.

Consistently working on a behavior we want to change promises us immense rewards, but until we try it, we doubt that it will work. Fortunately, if we go to enough meetings, we'll learn from the stories of our friends. They have experienced profound changes in their lives. We can have what they have found. It's guaranteed.

I can change any part of me that I really want to. Today is as good a day as any to begin the process.

SEPTEMBER

We get so bogged down in worldly things, we don't
understand that we're here for a spiritual quest.
—Oprah Winfrey

Those of us in recovery are perhaps luckier than most;
we have learned that our journey is spiritual. We have
come to believe that we each have a special mission and
that a Higher Power travels every step with us. However,
we can get bogged down. We can get upset by the experiences that come to us hour by hour, forgetting they are
part of our unfolding divine life.

Because we are human and imperfect, we forget that
we are in God's care at every moment. We also forget
that the people who share our lives now are helping us
learn the lessons we need for this stage of our development. Some people will leave us and others will join us
when the time is right. The plans have been made. All
we have to do is show up and peacefully trust that God
is in charge.

I am here for a purpose bigger than I might imagine.
God's guidance will be clear if I follow
my inner voice throughout this day.

Whether one has a natural talent or not, any learning period requires the willingness to suffer uncertainty and embarrassment.
—Gail Sheehy

We are all multitalented, but if we grew up in dysfunctional families, we may have failed to understand this. Households encumbered by tension, conflict over values or expectations, and confusion about roles of family members kept nurturing to a minimum. We grew up shortchanged. Fortunately, it is never too late to develop the talents that lie within us.

This recovery program will nurture our talents; the friends we make here will help us understand our worth. As we attempt the "new," we'll be helped along by the support of our Higher Power who promises to love, guide, and care for us.

I have the talent to do whatever I need to today if I let God and my friends help me.

Don't waste your time hating a failure.
—Clarissa Pinkola Estés

We are members of the human community. We make mistakes as we trek through this forest. We must remember that our mistakes offer us opportunities for new understanding. If we lived without error, our lives would be static, unchanging. Our emotions remind us that we are very much alive.

Self-hatred has been common among us. Anger, resentment, remorse, and terror are likewise familiar. Emotions will always play key roles in our lives. They can inspire us to action; they can also impede us. One of the most important lessons of recovery is knowing when to act and when to be still, when to forgive ourselves and when to feel shame, when to let go and when to take charge.

Deciding to move ahead instead of being shamed by a failure is evidence that we are recovering.

I will accept my failures today as part of my humanity and part of my education. I am here to learn.

There is a purpose for our existence which, at times, transcends human understanding.
—Aphrodite Matsakis

In the midst of our pain-filled past, few of us believed there was purpose to our lives. Most moments were frantically lived and accompanied by burning dread. How long has it been since we felt that way? What a changed perspective we have cultivated now that we are clean and sober!

We may not feel entirely safe every minute of every day. Old habits are not easily replaced. But we are coming to believe that it is no accident that we are in this program. The more we hear that our lives have purpose, the more comfortable we are with this understanding. As we progress through the Steps, it becomes easier to see the contribution past experiences made to current circumstances. Every piece has played its part, and we continue to evolve.

I am fulfilling a greater purpose given to me by God.
I may not understand my role today,
but it will become clear in time.

*Never pass up an opportunity to tell your loved
ones you love them.*
—*Sharon Walters*

We all know how wonderful it feels to be told we are
loved. As children, however, some of us seldom heard
this. And as adults we may have been in relationships
that didn't nurture us. We, too, may have trouble telling
other people how much we care. So often we imitate the
very behaviors we have grown accustomed to, even if
they are self-defeating.

We are learning through this program that we can
develop new behaviors. We are also learning to be patient
with ourselves when our learning curve is longer than
we had anticipated. Old patterns are not easily broken.
Fortunately, we are surrounded by wonderful friends and
caring sponsors who will help us work on the behaviors
we want to change.

Through the program we are learning that God's main
lesson involves learning how to give and receive love.
Initially we may have to act as if we love others. We may
have to force the words. But we will grow comfortable
with loving others.

*I will share my love with a friend or a relative today.
My need to give love may even exceed
the other person's need to receive it.*

My daughter has changed my life completely. For the first time I have stepped out of myself and given absolute, unconditional love to someone.
—Robyn Halsema

Deciding to step outside of ourselves, whether to love another person or to focus less on ourselves, is healthy. Being obsessed with ourselves, which we alcoholics and addicts tend to do, exaggerates every element of our lives, making it nearly impossible for us to maintain a balanced, healthy perspective.

Our self-consciousness and self-absorption isolate us. The more our attention centers on us, the less we grow in our understanding of how life is designed to unfold. Our growth suffers when we cut ourselves off from the other people who are in our lives to act as our teachers.

We will learn much about who we are and what we are here to do when we join with other people, and express our gratitude and love for their presence in our lives.

I can resist the temptation to isolate myself today.
Expressing even a small token of love or
gratitude to another woman will give me
peace and a measure of health.

I find myself wondering whether serenity is really attainable for women with small children.
—Mary Casey

Serenity is a state of mind. Children, animals, co-workers, careers, traffic, ringing phones, bad weather, drinking partners—all can steal our serenity if we let them. Even beautiful weather and loving companions can't guarantee serenity. Deciding to free our minds of the clutter that keeps us agitated is what assures our serenity.

Focusing on our Higher Power and seeking guidance will bring us peace. Even during the most troubling times, we can be at peace if we quiet our minds, focus on the Spirit within us, and remember that our lives are uniquely purposeful. We are needed; we have a specific role to play; in the stillness we can best decipher our particular part.

In the midst of havoc I can find the stillness, if that's my desire.

*Education is a private matter . . . and has little to
do with school or college.*
—Lillian Smith

Every experience educates us in some respect. Whether
these experiences cause us pain or joy, they teach us
about life. Some philosophers believe that our whole
reason for being is to become more enlightened about
the nature of the human and the divine.

Our responses to every circumstance we encounter
can instruct us about our inner self. Paying attention to
how we act and, more important, react increases our
understanding of who we are at specific moments. Taking
charge of those reactions is always possible; it demon-
strates willingness to "channel" our education.

Does it really matter why we are here? All of us have
been called to participate in this life. Growing in acceptance that all matters concerning us are like books to
be read gives us confidence that no experience will be
beyond our capacity to absorb.

*I eagerly anticipate what I will learn
about myself today. I have been called
to this moment. I am here.*

To change a behavior, we must become willing to experience a certain degree of discomfort.
—Marie Lindquist

Many of us believe that all our problems are someone else's fault. If others were more understanding, less critical, easier to love, we'd be happier, we think. But that's not true, and we're lucky it's not. If our happiness were tied to others' whims, we'd be happy far less often.

To have more happiness and security in our lives, we may have to change how we act. That's not always easy. Old behaviors are like old shoes: comfortable; they fit. But when happiness eludes us too often, we must look to ourselves for the remedy. The changes we may need to make won't be comfortable at first; they may pinch the ego like a tight shoe pinches the toes.

But relying on our Higher Power to keep us willing to change makes the transition possible. What once pinched will feel comfortable in time. Let's trust.

Today I'll release my impatience and keep my mind on the Serenity Prayer. My happiness is up to me.

I believe we all have a purpose in this life, and each day is a step in the journey toward achieving that purpose.

—Kathy McGraw

It is not always easy to remember that each of us has a unique purpose, one that is unfolding every moment of our lives. Many of our days seem lacking in excitement, devoid of momentous decisions or undertakings. Periods of our lives may seem to have evaporated: for example, we may recall nothing of our elementary school years or of parts of an earlier marriage or a painful relationship.

Trusting that our lives have purpose changes us. As our understanding deepens, we feel empowered and far more conscious of the opportunities our Higher Power offers us every day. We begin to see that every experience is purposeful.

We are here by assignment. Our homework is to learn and change, if necessary. We may never fully know our purpose, but with God's help we will trust how our lives are unfolding.

I may not understand all that is happening in my life at the present, but if I trust that my Higher Power is helping me to fulfill my purpose, I can accept the experience.

Instead of worrying about being different from others, I will love myself for being unique.
—Kelley Vickstrom

Where did we learn to compare ourselves with other women? Why is the process so seductive? We seldom measure up, in our eyes. Every woman we see, at first glance, seems smarter or wittier, and certainly more attractive. Self-doubt sets in again and again. Those few times we "win" the comparison test, we feel smug, but the victory is short-lived because another woman soon enters our space.

Meditating often about the gift of uniqueness that our birth guaranteed will bring us closer to understanding that gift. Why would God have made us all unique unless we were here to handle a very special assignment? At first this may not seem realistic. But think for a moment of the women you know in recovery. Are they setting identical goals for their lives? Do they think and act exactly alike? Our lives may be complementary and we may be walking similar paths, but our assignments are unique. God needs each of us for the divine picture to be whole.

I am who I need to be to fulfill my role in this divine world. What I have to offer is important.

*If we are to realize a peaceful, spiritual awareness,
there are mental practices we must engage in.*
—Margaret R. Stortz

To some people, having a meaningful life means being
busy all the time. While it's true that we need activities
that get us outside of ourselves, we can easily become
too busy. While using alcohol and other drugs, many of
us left too many projects unfinished. Perhaps we drifted,
making resolutions to change, to work, to accomplish a
goal, but never succeeding.

It's not surprising that we feel we must make up for
lost time now. The problem with this approach is that we
need to be still, with a quiet mind, to know the peace of a
truly meaningful life.

We have to make a habit of becoming quiet. We need
to practice freeing our minds of the thoughts that compete for our attention. In silence will come our knowledge of God. Our serenity and security reside in our quiet
moments.

*I can still my mind and know
God's presence and will for me today.*

*There comes a time in everyone's recovery when
we must begin to focus on wellness.*
—Julie B.

We have admitted we have a disease. We have also
agreed to get help. We address our disease by doing the
maintenance necessary to stay clean and sober—going
to meetings, calling our sponsor, reading recovery literature, and staying away from slippery places.

Cultivating wellness is the next step in our process.
Being free of hangovers isn't really wellness, even though
we feel much better. Being well means being fit physically, mentally, and spiritually. That comes from eating
healthy food, exercising regularly, getting enough rest,
and seeking the advice of professionals if mental or physical problems arise.

Before we stopped using our drugs of choice, we
couldn't comprehend what wellness meant. Each sober
day that we eat right and exercise moves us toward a more
rewarding life. That's wellness.

*I can stay clean and sober with a little effort.
And I can be well in mind, body, and spirit
with a little extra effort today.*

Sharing secrets requires trust. Accepting secrets requires an open heart.
                                   —*Kathleen Tierney Andrus*

Sometimes we feel so different, so out-of-place with our co-workers, siblings, or even friends. Self-consciousness overwhelms us when we hide parts of ourselves from other people, fearing they'd reject us if they knew who we really were. Living in fear and isolation with our secrets gives others far too much power over us. We're not comfortable when we try and hide so much of ourselves.

If we take notice, we'll see that at least one woman at every Twelve Step meeting risks her anonymity to talk about a dark area of her life. She is a wonderful example to us. Our acceptance of her heals her. Her sharing with us begins our own healing process.

Accepting the secrets a friend needs to share
today will help her heal. I will benefit too.
My secrets will no longer reign so powerful.

*Maturity doesn't come with age or intellectual
wisdom, only with love.*
—Ruth Casey

We may have thought being mature meant being
"grown-up." This meant acting rationally, showing good
judgment, no longer exhibiting childish behavior. It's
doubtful that we ever considered the expression of love
as an act of maturity. However, we are learning that the
key to sustained growth is the ability to love one another
and ourselves.

It seems so much easier to focus on others' faults than
on their assets. In childhood we learned to compete with
our classmates, and this taught us to be critical of one
another. No teacher tested us on how we expressed love;
rather, we worked on spelling and multiplication tables,
and we were pitted against other students for the gold
stars.

Now we are discovering how much more comfortable
life is when we all get gold stars. We are handling every
situation more sanely now that we have realized the gift
of serenity that accompanies our expression of love.

*My growth, my maturity in this program,
can best be measured by my attitude today.
Am I loving, or am I still competing with others?*

When I feed on resentments and anger, I am giving someone else rent-free space in my head.
—Kathy Kendall

Becoming consumed by our emotions is all too familiar. It was a favorite pastime before we got clean and sober, and it still may "own" us. Much to our dismay, sponsors remind us that we're getting a payoff or we wouldn't continue the practice. They also tell us it's never too late to give it up.

We can begin immediately. Let's breathe in the positive. It takes the same effort as dwelling on resentments, and the outcome is so much healthier. Let's bring our blessings to mind first. Breathe in the images of friends and the smiles we share. Breathe in the image of our Higher Power and those comforting arms. Breathe in the bright light of healing that is the program's gift. Breathe in the peace that comes with knowing all is finally well.

Giving our minds over to loving images heals us. The hurts of the past can reach us no more if we breathe in the good.

I will breathe in my Higher Power today.
I will dwell on the safety and serenity of my journey.

*When you really understand the fact of separate
realities, you will stop spending so much time and
energy trying to change the reality of others.*
—Jane Nelsen

What makes us want to control others, not just their actions but their opinions too? Do our personal views need the validation of everyone for us to feel adequate?

Coming to believe that we all have valid perspectives on every experience is akin to coming to believe that there is a Higher Power in charge of our lives. It takes willingness to suspend our assumptions and adopt the principles of this program.

It's liberating, even exhilarating, to realize that we all see situations a bit differently. It's like going from a black-and-white picture to seeing the world in full color. Our experiences are enriched as we view them with new attitudes.

*How I see my experiences today is up to me;
how my friends see theirs is up to them.
My view may complement theirs, but it's mine, solely.*

Almost everyone wants something for nothing.
—*Marsha Sinetar*

Bargains attract. Finding a good value excites us, and we share the news quickly. Wanting anything for free is human nature perhaps. However, many of us have had to learn again and again that you get what you pay for. This is true of human interactions too.

Why do we think that others will be there for us if we aren't available for them? Having friends means being a friend, even if it's time-consuming. Although friendship's rewards are indisputable, we still tend to wait, letting the other person make the first move. Getting the other person to commit first reduces our effort, perhaps, but we will still receive according to what we give.

Knowing and utilizing this principle simplifies our lives. Once we master it, we never forget it. And what we bring to our relationships will be given back to us.

I am willing to give to others what
I want in return today.
Their efforts will match my own.

Celebrate your life and hear your spirit sing.
—*Elisabeth L.*

"What's to celebrate?" some people ask. We all get our fill of the cynics. Their negativity can weigh down our spirits. But we don't have to let them control how we see our lives or theirs. To keep our own perceptions positive, it helps to detach from the naysayers. We will improve our chances if we consciously focus on gratitude for even the tiny blessings rather than on whatever might be wrong.

Becoming grateful is the strongest, safest means of feeling good now that we are in recovery. Not only does it readily alter our mood, but it changes our perspective on every detail of our lives. To be thankful rather than thankless is a small price to pay for unqualified happiness coupled with serenity.

We've all known people who radiate a singing spirit. They love life, themselves, and others. We seek out their company. We can be like those people for the travelers sharing our journey. Let's do it!

I will practice gratitude today
and be a blessing in everyone's life.

Sharing is healing.
—*Cathy Stone*

It's not easy to share the intimate details of our lives. We have guarded our secrets for years. But now it's suggested that we tell our secrets to people whose names we barely know. That's certainly not the way we were raised, and listening to others reveal their awful truths startles us initially. However, we can't help but notice how much better than us other people seem to feel. We eventually understand that the more we open up, the less encumbered we'll feel by the past.

The magic in sharing our experience, strength, and hope with others is hard to define. We simply know that when we do it, we feel relieved of our burden and we help another woman feel less isolated. We have come together because we want to get well.

I will make sure I'm not keeping something
to myself today that's causing me pain.
Whoever I share it with will be helped too.

*Each friend represents a world in us, a world
possibly not born until they arrive.*

—Anaïs Nin

We are surrounded by people who are necessary for
our development. That's a startling revelation perhaps.
We don't even like everybody in our life! How can we
need them? But we do. Our Higher Power clearly under-
stands our purpose and our needs, and ushers into our
lives those people who will help us grow and change and
contribute. It sounds mysterious initially, but when we
get accustomed to the idea, we are relieved. Each person
will teach us something we need to know about life and
about ourselves.

Our individual character is growing, changing,
maturing. Our understanding of others and our experiences deepen with each unfolding event. The world
is ever-changing. By design, not coincidence, we will
befriend those people who need us just as we need them.

*I am where I need to be.
My friends and associates need me as I need them.
We are moving and growing in concert.*

When I am lonely, I try to think of angels.
—Betty MacDonald

We need comfort when we feel lonely. Loneliness is often coupled with fear. We wonder, "Can I handle what faces me today?" Often we think we can't. But we don't ever have to face any situation alone or handle any painful relationship in isolation. The "angels" who guide and protect us are as close as our thoughts.

Twelve Step programs give us the freedom to define our Higher Power in any way that suits us. Believing our Higher Power is an angel satisfies our need to have someone watching over us, protecting us wherever we are, loving us despite our failings.

We are nurtured or harmed by the thoughts we carry in our minds. Imagining an angel or a ring of angels to walk us through each day relieves our loneliness and dissipates our fears.

I have a friend in my Higher Power.
We'll be together throughout this day.

*Life has lessons to teach. We can remember them
and share them with others, or we can forget them
and have to learn them again.*
—Jan Pishok

What we are destined to learn in this life will keep pre-
senting itself until we start remembering. Each experience is a minute part of the big picture that's unfolding.
We will receive the information we need, again and
again if necessary. Let's give up our fear about where
we are going and how we'll get there. We are in caring,
capable hands. We will get to the right destination on
time.

In this program we are invited to share with other
women what our experiences have taught us. What better
way to recall, and thus relearn, what we have been taught
than to tell another about it. Every Twelve Step program
is specifically designed to simplify our lives. The Steps
coach us through every situation, and they never shame
us for needing reminders of our lessons.

*I will help others through sharing my own
experiences today. In the process, I'll recapture
the essence of the lessons I have learned.*

Time spent attempting to change others affords little time for personal change.
— Georgette Vickstrom

We must be willing to change, or we wouldn't be reading these words right now. However, being willing to change is often easier than doing it. One of the biggest changes most of us need to make is learning to let others be who they are, regardless of who we want them to be. Most of us think our lives would be far smoother and more productive if only other people lived up to our standards. How wrong we are!

If we could change others as we wish, we would live far less enlightened lives. In fact, we discover opportunities for personal development in our interactions with the people who frustrate us so. The irony is that we wish they'd change, but if they did, we wouldn't experience the growth we deserve.

I will enhance my growth today by letting others be who they are and working on myself.

We can trust in the constancy of one thing—time will always move forward, taking us away from the old and gently guiding us to the new.

—Amy E. Dean

It's human nature to want the pleasurable experiences to last forever and the painful ones to leave immediately. But we can't move through anything faster than the hands of the clock will allow. A better response to our circumstances, regardless of their flavor, is acceptance that God has put a lesson in them for us and we can't adequately judge the long-term value of any of our experiences.

Nothing lasts forever. The slogan "This, too, shall pass" promises us the emotional relief we need when times are hard. Time is our friend, always, even when we don't like the lesson. We do get what we need, when we need it.

I am on track. What comes to me today is something my Higher Power says I'm ready for. The time is always right.

I used to lament, "I'm drowning in a sea of apathy!" Now I rejoice in real emotion—mine, yours, all of ours.

—D. M. G.

Many of us were used to shutting down our feelings. We gladly used whatever "medication" was at our disposal: alcohol, pills, even food. We weren't fussy. But emotions need to be acknowledged, so ours never really went away, even though we refused to feel them. They hid. Now they are back.

Handling anger, sadness, fear, and even joy takes patience. Feelings indicate what we are thinking. They aren't necessarily good or bad, but they do influence our actions. Being aware of them, and understanding that they are within our control, helps us accept them, understand them, absorb them, release them. Feelings let us know that we care, that we're alive and aware of the others in our lives. Let's use our feelings, not hide them away or let them use us.

I prefer joy, but I will acknowledge every feeling that surfaces today. My feelings mirror my thoughts.

I alone can do it. But I can't do it alone.

—*Anonymous*

We're the luckiest women alive because we don't have to do anything alone! Whether we have a new assignment to tackle, a new relationship to cultivate, or a new boss to please, we'll never fail as long as we rely on the program, our sponsors, and our Higher Power.

That doesn't mean we won't have trying times and some failures. But the companionship we need for handling the difficult periods will never be denied us. Perhaps we think it will. Maybe that's why we try to do too much alone.

We didn't end up in this Twelve Step program as the result of living peaceful, productive lives. We're here because we got scared. Our lives weren't working. And they won't work now if we insist on doing it alone. This is our second chance. Let's take it.

*I will seek the support I need from friends
and God today. I'll have a good day because of this.*

I've finally realized that it's not happiness we should search for in this life, but the ability to survive life's stresses.
—Kay Lovatt

We deserve happiness, but focusing on personal happiness as our sole purpose gives us only fleeting satisfaction. Sponsors and friends remind us that helping others find joy and love gives us more lasting happiness than all the selfish pursuits that attract us can give.

Our periods of happiness are interspersed with the struggles that come with being human. We might have thought that getting clean and sober would eliminate all our problems, but fortunately that's not the case. Problems, after all, offer us opportunities to rely on God's guidance and comfort, and that's the key lesson most of us need to learn.

Twelve Step programs are changing millions of lives. Those of us who rely on them are learning to give to God the "work" that belongs to God, keeping for ourselves only what needs to be done by us.

I will not be given anything I can't handle today if I let God help me.

*It is the long stretch of time that gives us our
viewpoint.*
—Florida Scott-Maxwell

In the heat of an experience, our emotions own us. Hurt
feelings, anger, or fear pushes away the rational expla-
nation of what occurred. It's often not until hours or
maybe days later that we understand the dynamics of
that moment.

Wishing we could gather all the facts immediately is
understandable. It might save us from losing control of
our emotions. But learning to step back before responding to an experience takes discipline.

Hindsight is perhaps our best teaching tool. We can
review the past and see how every experience, even the
most painful, has added to our development. Trusting
that the same will be true of whatever appears on our
horizon today relieves us of the need to worry and over-
react. Since we know we'll understand in due time, let's
relax now.

*I remember some difficult periods that
benefited me. If something troubles me today,
perhaps I can trust that it, too, is for my good.*

Wisdom lets us know that the key is not to judge,
but to love and nurture.
                                        —Jane Nelsen

Freeing our minds of judgment is far more difficult than
we'd imagined. It often seems our minds fill up by themselves. That's not true, of course. We cannot always be
in control of everything, but we are always in charge of
our thoughts.

Harboring only loving thoughts may seem beyond our
capabilities at first. So did living without alcohol and
other drugs, yet we are managing that one day at a time.
Nothing is too much for us to handle if we make the effort
moment by moment. Making the decision to "think love"
is doable. The proof is in the practice.

How I feel about myself today is tied to
how I decide to feel about others.
My love of them will help me love myself.

OCTOBER

The first step on the spiritual path needs to be the cultivation of a lively sense of wonder.

—Alison Davis

The tiniest elements in the universe are often the most beautiful. A single violet in a field of wildflowers, birds in their vibrant splendor, exotic fish in the ocean, insects seen and unseen—all leave little doubt that a creative hand has played its part.

On a more personal scale, our bodies, our physical attributes, our ability to feel and think and act give us cause to marvel. Life in all its forms is undoubtedly miraculous.

That each of us is alive to read these words is a miracle too. For many of us, death through accident, overdose, or a partner's violence was little more than a thought or moment away. It is not by accident that we survived. We have a role to play in the unfolding lives of those who share our time and space. We are part of their miracle.

Seeing the miracles in my path today
takes nothing more than being attentive.
They are everywhere I look.

As our spirituality grows and changes, we can
allow our image of God to change.
—Ruth Schweitzer-Mordecai

As children we may have pictured God as a man with long hair, a beard, and flowing robes. For some of us, that image may still be the most comfortable. As adults, however, we have the freedom to define God however we wish. Hearing our sisters share their perceptions of a Higher Power has given us the courage to create Whoever we need.

God may not even be an image some days but only a feeling. The brilliant light reflecting off the drops of morning dew, the delicate hum of the hungry hummingbird, or the radiance of an American Beauty rose may whisper of the presence of God. A passage we read in a timeworn book may also remind us of God's reality. Whether it's a feeling, a few words, a specific image, or a profound experience, God will be as real in our lives as we are willing to allow.

The more I believe in God today,
the easier will be my journey. I am not alone.
The Presence is always with me.

*When we live in a place for too long, we grow
dull. We don't notice what is around us.*
— Natalie Goldberg

Why is it so hard to be aware of our surroundings?
What occupies our minds? Most of us can't adequately
answer these questions. We aren't even aware that we
are *not aware*. Ego has us trapped and not against our
will. Being unaware has simply become our way of life.
Unseeing, we move through the minutes, the places,
and the experiences that wear our name, noticing only
ourselves.

Our journey is unique. The specific path we travel is
trod by no one but us. No detail is without meaning; every
moment, every person, every object has significance for
us. Our task is to take notice and be grateful. What we
need to know, what we are here to learn, is evident in the
many tiny elements in our lives. Let's not miss them.

*Looking thoroughly around me today will reveal
God's messages. Nothing has been left to chance.*

*How often in my loneliness I have said things I
didn't sincerely mean just to please another.*
—Mary Norton Gordon

Our desire to bond with others can be intense. In our
youth we followed the pack, even when we knew we'd
be punished after we got home. Our need to belong
hasn't lessened in adulthood. Before getting clean and
sober, we formed alliances with many people who didn't
share our view of life. We relied on these attachments
because loneliness was too overwhelming and anyone
was better than no one.

Today we know that the Twelve Step program has given
us what we needed all along. What a lifesaver! And all
that's been asked of us in return is our presence at meetings and our willingness to let other people really know
us. It's so simple. We're surrounded by women who want
to share our lives, who have similar stories, who searched
as we did in all the wrong places. These bonds are offered
sincerely.

*If I feel myself ready to go along with something
to which I don't agree, it's my cue to call a sponsor
or a friend for the intimacy I crave.*

We are all diamonds in the rough.
—Roseann Lloyd

We tend to exaggerate our own imperfections and glorify other women's strengths. In reality, we are all imperfect yet quite good enough. Since getting clean and sober and joining this sisterhood of recovery, we have been given the tools for smoothing the rough edges of our character. Becoming a real gem is within our reach.

How do we begin? It's important to keep our efforts simple. Because we have so much we want to change, many of us try to change everything about ourselves overnight. The result is overwhelming frustration. We became who we are now over many years of reckless living. We must be realistic. Committing to one tiny change a day is enough to focus on. And it's more than enough to eventually bring about the overall changes we seek.

When we accept that who we are right now is okay with God, we'll also accept the pace of our progress in becoming who we want to be.

Watching my facets begin to sparkle can make each day a thrill to live. I'll appreciate the opportunities to polish my rough edges today.

Wisdom not gained from within is only someone else's knowledge.
—Georgette Vickstrom

Now that we are clean and sober and working the Steps of this program, we have the opportunity to discover that we possess good judgment. Our sponsors can help us in this undertaking, but we need to be cautious.

Needing to be right is a common malady among alcoholics and addicts, and we have to take that into account when others try to help us make decisions. Just because we are surrounded by program people doesn't mean we'll always get good advice. On the contrary, we can expect a fair share of poor advice aggressively given. Using the Steps and the slogans will help us discern rather quickly what's valuable to us and what is not.

I will look to others for help when I need it;
however, I'll rely on my own judgment too.
My inner voice has my best interest at heart.

Women's bodies resonate spiritual messages.
Listen to them.
—Judi Hollis

Our bodies are so much more than what we see in the mirror. They house our soul. They house our history. Our bodies have long memories. All that has happened to them remains in them. We share our bodies with a spirit who is the source of our strength and knowledge.

Oftentimes the messages we get from the spirit are subtle. We barely sense them. When we're honest with ourselves, however, we admit that we know when our Higher Power has spoken. Some describe the contact as a pinch in the conscience, others as a clutching feeling in the stomach. Tension in the neck and shoulders may be how God gets your attention. The point is, we each must attune ourselves to God's special way of reaching us.

Why listen to these messages? Because our journey will be helped if we let God decide our path. We have a destiny to fulfill.

I will listen while my Higher Power
speaks to me today. I won't get off track
if I stay in tune with my body.

Healing begins with a state of mind.
                                        —Carol Sheffield

The mind gives birth to all our emotions and attitudes. Our anger, our sadness, our joy, our self-esteem are cultivated in the mind. What we tell ourselves, we become. Unfortunately, self-sabotage is often our habit. But whatever is done can be undone. That's the good news. And the same tool we used to beat ourselves up can be used to undo the harm. We have always been in charge of what we believe about ourselves. The assignment is to change our beliefs.

We can begin by creating positive affirmations and repeating them to ourselves every morning. We can follow this with a commitment to stop every negative thought once it starts. We will succeed with perseverance.

We are lucky, really. When it comes to negative self-talk, we're no different than other people. That we have a program to help us change our behavior is the luck. Let's relish our good fortune.

Healing begins with me today.
I'll only be as well as I tell myself I am.

It doesn't matter what we have done in the past.
—Melody Beattie

Shame about the past is not unusual, particularly for women like us. It isn't a productive feeling, however. Shame keeps us stuck, and we have joined this program to grow. Let's let the past go, accepting simply that it provided us with experiences that have pushed us to new heights of awareness. What we've learned from those experiences, if shared, will educate another soul who still suffers.

The twenty-four hours that lie ahead are our only concern now. We can make them productive, fulfilling, and peaceful if we honor each hour. The women and men who come to us today, the events that are triggered by their presence, and the attitude we harbor determine the fruitfulness of any moment. What a thrill to fully realize that our journey has a purpose and an intensity special to the particular lesson each of us needs.

I don't have to let the past hinder me any longer.
I can be free of it, if that's my desire.

I can no longer afford the luxury of blaming others for my choices.
—Jan Pishok

We may long for the years when we felt free to blame other people for our troubled lives. But living so irresponsibly didn't benefit us. While it might seem overwhelming to shoulder the responsibility for all our choices, every action and reaction, this is the path to emotional maturity. That's why we are here.

Being accountable for our lives builds our self-esteem. When we first make the decision to be in charge, we may think the responsibility is more than we can handle. But with each conscious choice, we discover our strength and our resolve being enhanced.

We do want emotional, mental, and spiritual health. That's why we sought recovery. That's why we have adopted these Twelve Steps as our guidelines for living. Using them in all our daily affairs promises us the real luxury of growth and freedom from fear.

I am in charge of my choices today.
God will never steer me wrong.

What honest heart denies that many delights are
based on the premise that others will not, even
cannot, do what you do?
                                    —Florida Scott-Maxwell

Seldom do our successes come easy, so taking pride in
our accomplishments is appropriate. But being grateful
for our Higher Power's help is even more appropriate.
This partnership assures us of success, even when we
think we have done it alone.

Our culture admonishes us to be self-reliant, independent, strong. None of these qualities is inherently wrong,
but they leave us shortchanged. We also need to depend
on God, to be vulnerable, and to look to other people for
support and love, just as they look to us.

No one can do anything in exactly the way we do. And
that empowers us. We bring our unique perception to
every undertaking, and this vision, coupled with God's
participation, interprets and guides our understanding
and our response.

I have an assignment today. Every day, in fact,
I am doing God's work. I'll have help if I accept it.

The more we give, the more we receive.
—Veronica Ray

We blame human nature for our desire to get rather than give. There are people who focus on giving, however. We see them at meetings. We probably wonder how these people do it and why. We'd be wise if we quit wondering and simply tried to imitate their behavior.

We've heard the advice "Give it away in order to keep it" often at meetings. In the early days we failed to understand the message. We can't use that excuse anymore. Our insecurity, or perhaps our stinginess, wants to hang on to our possessions, our well-being, our understanding of "how it works." The paradox is that we'll lose what we have if we don't share it with others.

Every episode in our life is an opportunity to share the wisdom we have gained from living the principles of this program. It is no coincidence that we have been given this wisdom. Let's share it.

I will be willing to share what I have
learned with the others in my life today.
At least one of them needs what I can offer.

*We know our greatest anger, as well as our
deepest love, in our roles as daughters, sisters,
lovers, wives, and mothers.*
—Harriet Lerner

Denying our anger is not unusual. We were trained well
in our families to deny anger and repress other feelings,
such as love. We are suffering from the repercussions of
that training now.

It is okay to be angry, but how we deal with anger is
important. Using it against ourselves or to manipulate
others is not healthy. Acknowledging anger is the first
step to being free of it. That sounds easy, but if we were
raised to deny anger, admitting we feel it is risky. Our
sponsors and friends who share this program are role
models we can follow. There is a lot of hard work ahead of
us in recovery if we're angry. But if we weren't ready for it,
we wouldn't be here. We get the opportunities for growth
that we are prepared to handle. Let's trust our feelings
and share them all at last.

*It is safe to talk about my anger today.
I will be honest with those I can trust.
My happiness is tied to my honesty.*

Love is a powerful thing, but does it always kick in to save the day when you feel things are hopeless?

—*Chris DeMetsenaere*

When we first get into recovery, it is hard to understand love—how it feels, how to give it, and how to accept it. Most of us have used the pretense of loving someone as our excuse for trying to control that person. It can be painful to realize that genuine love means letting our friend or lover or child go, letting that person make decisions or mistakes independent of us. But each day we are given is time we can use to nurture this realization into acceptance.

As our understanding grows, so does our awareness that nothing is ever hopeless. We begin to see that love not only comforts and frees us, but also can soften the harsh edges of any brittle reality. Love is a choice we can make in any situation. But best of all, the more we focus on giving love away, the smoother our experiences will be.

I will offer my love freely today without falling into the seductive trap of control. I will remember the paradox: to have genuine love for another person means to let go of that person.

Strangely, it was comforting to me when I read that squirrels forget where they hide about half their nuts.
—Ruth Casey

We sometimes set unreasonably high standards for ourselves. Instead of being content with average, we think we must be perfect or we don't count. The problem is that none of us can be perfect in every endeavor. To be human is to be fallible. And that's okay, even though we don't often believe it.

God doesn't expect perfection. How often have we been reminded of that since joining this program? What God does expect is that we do our best and do it lovingly. Whether we are at work, at home cooking dinner for the family, or at the bedside of an ailing friend or partner, we need only give the task our focused attention and willing heart. The joy we feel as the result of our efforts will convince us that we have been as close to perfect as we need to be.

I will do the best I can today if I am determined to be attentive to the task at hand and loving in my attitude.

I always have a choice: to learn from the lessons life offers me or to retreat into my lonely victim role.

—*Charlotte Kasl*

What a difference it makes in our journey to believe that every experience is an opportunity to grow and to heal the pain of being human. None of us travel this road unscathed. Our interactions are devastating on occasion, but we can survive them. And sharing how we did so can give other women hope and strength and healing when they most need it.

Luckily not every experience is hard or painful. Many moments every day are delightful. Sometimes the joy we feel and the laughter we share are simply the result of being grateful for our daily blessings. Our attitudes have far-reaching consequences in our lives. How we choose to interpret the actions of others determines how we feel. Our serenity doesn't have to be dependent on others' actions.

I will be as joyful as I choose today.
If I'm willing to accept assistance,
my Higher Power will help me make the choice.

*Our anxiety about clarifying what we think
and how we feel may be greatest in our most
important relationships.*
—Harriet Lerner

We want love and acceptance from everybody, especially our most intimate friends. Because we fear their judgment—or even worse, their rejection—we pale at the thought of letting them know who we really are, what we really think, how we really feel.

Yet when we don't let the important people in our lives know us fully, we never feel secure. We live in fear that they will leave us. Acknowledging that our happiness is this tentative can help us take the plunge into real honesty with others. What have we got to lose?

We couldn't have taken this risk of honesty before coming to this program of recovery. But here we have role models to look to, sponsors to talk to, and a Higher Power to pray to. We will be able to do what we couldn't do before, and our relationships will reflect it.

*I can risk letting my friends see the real me today.
My honesty, shared lovingly, won't send them away.*

The world has more depth in autumn. So, it
seems, does my soul.
—*Jane Nakken*

The earth prepares to rest when autumn comes. Trees shed their leaves, flowers drop their blooms, grass grows more slowly. This can be likened to our own periods of quiet contemplation when we outgrow old ideas and prepare for new direction in our life.

It's good that we have resting periods. We can't know where or how far we want to go if we haven't taken time to measure how far we have come. The fall of the year is a good time to do another Fourth Step inventory.

What's the point of repeated inventories? Sponsors tell us that growth is never ending and that we can direct it best if we clearly know where we are right now. The only certain way of knowing that is through careful assessment of who we are today. Let's stop and rest and contemplate our journey. Then let's plan for the next leg.

My quiet times will inspire my journey today.
I will be prepared for a new direction if that feels right.

*Creativity and self-expression are the keys which
open the door to my soul.*
—Betty MacDonald

Why do we find it so hard to believe that we are creative
and talented? Generally we look upon "artists" as being
far different from us. When we were young, we were encouraged to be ordinary, "like everyone else." Those who
dared to see the world differently were weird. Thus our
creative juices lay untapped.

But every spirit, by its very nature, is creative and talent
filled. Fortunately, the well of our creative spirits hasn't
run dry. We can prime the pump and bring them bub-
bling to the surface. The first step is to acknowledge our
creative potential.

The real gift of this journey is that hope has been
inspired in us. We hear the stories of how others have
changed and tapped into their creativity. We understand
it can happen to us too.

*Being willing to have my talents revealed is necessary
for it to happen. I will work on willingness today.*

Grace is when we notice the near-misses we survived instead of the wishes that didn't come true.

—Nancy Hull-Mast

We all have stories about the harrowing past: the times we woke up not knowing where we were, the open prescription bottle we couldn't remember emptying, the bashed-in fender, or the open front door of our home. How did we get from there to here? And why?

"There but for the grace of God…" is a saying that we come to appreciate when our mind finally clears. We were saved, many times. We have all read about people who weren't as lucky as we were. Curiously we wonder, "Why me?" Perhaps we should ponder, instead, what we can do with our lives now that we're here.

We have a unique contribution to make to our loved ones, or we wouldn't have come this far. The next step is to listen to our inner voice for guidance. We have a job to do. It's time to get on with it.

It's no accident that I am here.
I may not know what my job is today,
but God will help me understand.

*Recovery leads to self-knowledge, love, and joy.
Addiction leads to self-loathing, fear, and isolation. The choice is mine.*
                                            —Sarah Desmond

Having decided on a clean and sober life gives us opportunities we'd never have imagined. We're learning
how to love ourselves and appreciate other people. We're
learning that a Higher Power guides and protects us.
No one makes our decisions for us. We are free to go
back to the old life any time we want to. Each day offers
us a clean slate. We fill it in according to the principles
we live by. Making healthy choices regarding these
twenty-four hours becomes easier as we accumulate a
series of healthy days.

Occasionally we wonder why we chose a fearful, isolated life. Recovery was always available to us. We weren't
ready for it, however, and it's far more productive to trust
that we came to this program when the time was right.

*I choose how I live each day. Understanding that
makes the right choice more obvious.*

I didn't realize until recently that the emptiness inside was gone. It started to dissipate when I began cultivating a relationship with God.

—Cathy Stone

We spent our lives trying to fill the emptiness inside. We looked to drugs or food or relationships. For brief spells we may have felt filled up, but in the early morning hours the fear and loneliness generally returned. Why hadn't we learned about the hope that comes from having a relationship with God?

Everything looks different to us when we include a caring Higher Power in our picture. The terror dissipates when God is present. The torment over what decision to make is gone when God is consulted. Expanding our perspective to embrace the reality of God's existence changes even the tiniest details in our lives.

What a wonderful gift we have in this relationship with God. Our worries are gone, if we want them to be. Our emptiness is filled, if we want it to be. Our joy is complete, if we are ready.

My relationship with God
will answer all my questions today.

I must be prepared before the crisis comes.
                                                    —Ruth Humlecker

Being prepared for a crisis may seem like a negative outlook to some. After all, if we expect trouble, won't we get it? However, there is another way to think about preparation: it is a chance to make sure the tools of the program are easily accessible and familiar through use.

For example, one valuable tool is available when we give our lives and will to God. We can handle any situation if we let our Higher Power help carry our burdens. Another valuable tool is communicating regularly with a sponsor. We can avoid many disasters when we seek her advice, since her thinking is often clearer than our own.

Many crises result from our attempts to force other people to live according to our rules. Becoming willing, through the broad application of Step One, to accept our powerlessness over everybody else saves us from many conflicts. Unchecked conflicts are the stuff that crises are often made of.

The best preparation, of course, is believing that we'll never be given more that we can handle.

I am prepared to handle whatever comes
to me today. The program will see me through
every detail of my life.

Attitude and perspective are everything. Thus I see the glass as half full, not half empty.
—*Kathy Kendall*

Cynics rob themselves of the happiness they deserve. Sometimes we let them rob us of our happiness as well. Fortunately, our attitudes aren't up for grabs unless we relinquish ownership.

Developing a loving, positive attitude isn't difficult. If our family of origin was angry and opinionated, we may have gravitated toward a similar outlook. But with some effort we can follow the examples of people with a more positive outlook: good role models are easy to find in Twelve Step programs.

We'll discover that we can create a more accepting perspective. No one sees our experiences exactly as we do; each of us responds to life uniquely. We can come to understand this profound truth and willingly develop respect for all perspectives. When we accept that others' interpretations are right for them, and decide to see the positive rather than the negative in our own lives, we are promised true contentment.

*I can kick the negatives out of my life today
if that's my choice. How I look at any experience
depends on how I choose to see it.*

As a woman, I may err. Just for today I will cherish my humanness.
—Jan Pishok

Making mistakes is normal. We grew up in families where mistakes were common. Books have typos, announcers mispronounce names, coworkers forget meetings, friends overlook birthdays, gas tanks run dry. So why do we think we must be perfect?

Expecting more of ourselves than we do of others is common among women in recovery. We fear that if we're not perfection personified, we're not worthy! It may be that demanding parents and teachers helped instill this when we were young, but we don't have to continue cultivating it. Yet we do continue. Fortunately, it's never too late to change a habit, even one as ingrained as this.

Giving ourselves permission to be human and imperfect relieves us of a terrible burden. Truly believing that no one else is perfect either makes the prospect more acceptable.

Some of my actions will be errorless today, but many will fall short of perfection, just like everyone else's. I am as okay as I need to be.

So often I have listened to everyone else's truth and tried to make it mine.

—Liane Cordes

Being different from others was so painful in our youth. We wanted to belong, to look like our friends, to think like them, to be like them in every way. We wanted them to share our dreams and opinions. Rather than risk that they wouldn't, we mimicked them. Who were we? We seldom knew, because it depended on who we were with.

That is still a problem for many of us. Fortunately, our friends in this recovery program do not expect us to share their opinions unless they fit us too. Listening to another woman's truth honors her. Taking her truth as our own, when it isn't, dishonors both of us. This program teaches us respect if we are willing students. To be praised, rather than judged, for our integrity, even when it means we are different, is a refreshing and humbling experience.

I will listen to my truth today and respect everyone else's too. I am not here to judge, but to honor and love.

Find everyday reasons to dance.
                                        —Elisabeth L.

Just being alive is reason enough to dance, if we ponder it for a moment. It's not an accident that we lived through sometimes terrifying experiences. Nor is it accidental that we are in our current setting. We are needed by our friends, our family, even the strangers among us. Let's cherish our opportunities to be in the presence of these others today.

Our lives are akin to a ballet. While learning the steps, we may stumble a bit, but the dance needs us all. Let's never assume another person isn't necessary to our own performance. If she is here, we need her.

"How has this all happened?" we wonder. "How did I get here? Can I pull off my part?" Our doubts need not hinder us if we remember that we got here with help; we'll fulfill our role with the same ready help.

> *I can kick up my heels today and know*
> *that I can dance. All I need to do is*
> *listen for the music.*

There is magic in our souls. The adventure of recovery is finding that magic and allowing it to come forth.
—*Dudley Martineau*

Our lives are so different now that we are in recovery. The smallest problems used to plague us. Seldom did we know how to handle even minor conflicts. Our confidence waned. Faith was even more remote. Now our lives seem magical at times. How profoundly different each day, each experience looks to us now.

But where has the magic come from? How can a simple program with only a suggested set of guidelines change everything about our lives? Reading words like these, going to meetings, seeking the counsel of a sponsor on a regular basis, and making the Twelve Steps central to our lives is all the effort it takes. We discover that nothing overwhelms us anymore. And we have guardian angels who will direct every action if we so choose. There's the magic.

I will let the magic of this program work for me today. I won't be at a loss when I must come to any decision today.

*Clarifying my own values is an important
ingredient in my using the Serenity Prayer. From
that I have the "wisdom to know" the things I can
and cannot change about a situation.*

—Rose Casey

This program helps us discover our values. Doing a
moral inventory and then weighing our assets and shortcomings gives us clarity regarding the person we are and
the person we hope to become. Let's not be concerned
that we didn't know ourselves before. The past is past;
today is where our opportunities begin.

Today will offer us a host of experiences about which
we must make decisions, form judgments, take actions.
If we know our values, we will not be troubled by these
experiences. And yet living according to our values takes
practice. We were probably good at doing what others did
to fit in. Taking the risk of not fitting in is a profound decision that can benefit us in untold ways.

*My values will guide me as I decide what to do in
every situation I face today. Without this program,
I'd still be in constant quandaries.*

It is time to enter into
knots of fear
and watch them
uncurl into
waves of love.
                              —G. Carol

The fear that hinders most of us is due to our obsession to control the behavior of others. This fear, coupled with our compulsion to manage outcomes that are clearly beyond our control, keeps us stuck in situations that we need to grow beyond.

We're extremely fortunate to be part of this fellowship because we are surrounded by friends who understand our kind of fear and are willing to help us through scary times. We will have the opportunity to repay the favor many times over. We are all learning to handle fear and, thus, are discovering together that the risks we take in the company of one another prepare us for bigger challenges on our own. The empowerment that is guaranteed us will sustain our efforts as we take each new risk.

With the help of friends, I can feel my fears
and keep them in perspective. I will be able
to feel more love when I let the fears go.

Sometimes it seems I've spent my life trying to live up to others' expectations of me, and failing. I never thought much about pleasing myself. That would have been "selfish."
—JoAnn Reed

We can feel burdened, inadequate, and overwhelmed by expectations, even when they are our own. More often, however, the problem originates from outside ourselves. Before we got into the program, we may have been easily caught in the trap of other people's expectations because we didn't know who we really were. Now that we are in recovery, the Fourth Step offers us an opportunity to understand ourselves better, which in turn helps us to set our own goals. No longer must someone else's goals guilt us into action.

Getting to know real freedom from the expectations of others is a two-step process. First we need to see clearly which expectations are ours and which belong to someone else. Then we need to turn to our Higher Power for help in fulfilling our own expectations and only our own.

Before taking any action today I will pause to make certain I am fulfilling my expectations not someone else's. God will help me with this task.

NOVEMBER

In order to accept change and the suffering it
brings, we need to find meaning in it.
—Mary Norton Gordon

In the midst of upheaval, we may long for the security of the past. But when we recall earlier times, we realize change has always been nipping at our heels. We're reminded that we survived each change, and we gain confidence that we'll weather this storm too.

We don't have to suffer just because we are experiencing change. While change may stir our emotions, we can cultivate excitement for the change rather than fear of it. Further, we can use our memories of other changes and the fruits they bore as our inspiration now for relishing the opportunities every change offers us.

Change will come if God thinks it is time for us to stretch our talents and deepen our wisdom. It may be hard to keep that in mind when we feel the dread of change, but our memories will serve us if we'll let them.

Change is for my benefit, and my
Higher Power is my benefactor. I'll rejoice
if something new beckons to me today.

I truly want to be part of the solution, not part of the problem.
— *Kathy Kendall*

Honestly assessing how we perceive our experiences reveals how prone we are to create problems. Seeing the glass as half empty is a habit, perhaps one we can't imagine breaking. Fortunately, now we are surrounded by the good example of other people. Through listening at meetings we learn that the women we most admire understand our outlook. They have had it too.

We are in the company every day of women who have changed in the very ways we want to change. No matter how hopeless we feel at times, their very presence reminds us that we can do what they have done. Turning to their Higher Power was their solution. And that's ours too. We can turn to our Higher Power every time we begin to dwell on some experience that we've made into a bigger problem than it needs to be. Turning to our Higher Power becomes easier with practice, and in time, newcomers will admire our perspective, just as we have admired the perspective of others.

*I can emulate the good example of other people
today rather than getting stuck in a problem.
It's all in how I look at my opportunities.*

*I honor every woman who has strength enough to
step out of the beaten path when she feels that her
walk lies in another, strength enough to stand up
and be laughed at, if necessary.*

—Harriet Hosmer

It's never been easy for women to dare to be different.
The messages that surround us seldom encourage us to
pursue unconventional passions. Fortunately, we who
are on this recovery journey get personal guidance from
our Higher Power and our sponsors as we pursue the
opportunities that beckon to us along new paths. We
know, perhaps better than most, that we'll be protected
and directed each step of the way.

We have gathered to make this journey together. We
have needed each other all along; now we have each other
every step of the way. We will find the strength we need
from one another. We will joyfully follow our passions
and find the happiness we deserve.

*I am on my way to fulfillment. Even when
my path veers away from others, I'm in the
company of my Higher Power and my friends.*

*I will never be able to feel the love someone wants
to give to me unless I am loving myself.*
—Betty MacDonald

Loving ourselves sounds so simple, but how do we do it? Learning more about who we are is a good first step. The Fourth Step inventory leaves little doubt about who we are, providing we are vulnerably honest. And after acknowledging who we are, we can begin the process of accepting what we can and changing what we need to. Self-love is the reward for carefully doing our work.

The shame we feel for the person we think we are makes it hard to believe others could love us. Getting a more balanced view of ourselves changes our perspective. It becomes easier to love ourselves when we acknowledge how hard we are working to change. We want love. We deserve to be loved. We must be the initiators.

*Loving myself may take effort, but if I
remember that I'm doing the best I can,
and then do it, today will be easier.*

*We are following a mystery we can never
understand until we experience it.*
—Jacquelyn Small

How many times have we exclaimed, "If only I had known that was going to happen!" We think we'd be better off knowing the future before it arrives. It's quite by design that we don't, however. We are given all the information we need when we need it, just as we are given the experiences that fit the plan that God has for our lives.

It helps to reflect a few moments each time we fear the unknown. We'll easily recall that much of the past confused us at first, but all of our experiences dovetailed appropriately, bringing us here, now. And our lives no longer look mysterious given the gift of hindsight.

We are on a charted course to a planned destination. We will understand our role in this life when the proper time presents itself. Until then, let's enjoy the mystery.

*My life is special and fully understood
by my Higher Power. I'll get glimpses
of understanding as I need them today.*

There is an intuitive core at the depth of your being.
—Helene Lerner-Robbins

Deep within ourselves, we know much more than we think. We haven't yet learned to tap this inner source of wisdom, but now that we have found this spiritual program, lessons will be forthcoming. This means that each of us is fully capable of understanding the best way to attain a serene life. Within our souls lie all questions and a path to their answers. Our self-centeredness commonly blocks the information that's trying to rise to our awareness. However, when we can keep our ego small, our humility large, we'll understand clearly why we are here, what we need to know, what we have to do.

When we are frustrated, it's hard to believe that we have the wisdom we need within us. We race from one meager option to another, finding no solution. But if we still the mind, the information we seek will bubble forth. Hard to believe? Not once we've tried it. Hard to remember? Not with enough practice.

I am wise. The knowledge I need today
will rise to my mind's eye.

Learning and maturation in the life of the spirit cannot be hurried, and as in physical and intellectual development, a great deal depends on our readiness.
—Mary McDermott Shideler

We are ready for a spiritually directed life. It took us many stress-filled years to get here, and a number of us survived harrowing experiences during the journey. Even when we didn't understand our search, we wanted security and knowledge of how to live. But we didn't know we were on this path.

Now that we're here, some of us expect to know joy, serenity, and security in a flash. For a very few, a profound spiritual experience happens quickly. But most of us have to wait and work on our willingness and readiness to follow the path that leads to God.

How do we become willing? The Steps will guide our actions and our thoughts, and make us ready to receive the blessings we seek.

God will recognize my desire for peace
by the way I act today. I will have peace
if I treat others peacefully.

*Death, I now see, may not come when I am
eighty-five and weary. . . . It will come whenever
it damn well pleases.*

—Joyce Wadler

Seldom do we pause to absorb the fact of our mortality
thoroughly. The unexpected death of an acquaintance
can shock us into this realization, but it's far better to
remember that all we have is now.

Using this recovery program to guide our thinking
and our behavior helps us live more in this moment.
The slogan "One day at a time" specifically addresses
our need to be here, now. Deciding that our destiny is in
the reliable hands of our Higher Power gives us a respite
from worrying about the future. The miracle of our specific recovery, particularly in light of all those who don't
receive the gift, should convince us that our journey is by
design. So is our death.

*I have today. I'll make the most of it
and leave the future to God.*

*Because thoughts come from the inside, and not
from the outside, what we think determines what
we see.*
                                        —*Jane Nelsen*

It's difficult to remember that we are in charge of our
thoughts and thus what we experience. But it's also exciting to contemplate all the changes we can make by
focusing on positive thoughts.

Perhaps we can try this together. Put this book aside for
a moment and look closely at your surroundings. Think
about how lucky you are to have a place to sit, a peaceful
moment to contemplate your life. Think grateful thoughts
about your friends and family. Notice how you feel when
you have pleasant thoughts running through your mind.

Our lives are as fruitful, hopeful, and peaceful as we
choose. The show that goes on in our minds and is acted
out in our experiences has been produced and directed
by us.

*I am eager to experience my life today. Knowing
that it will match my thoughts is exhilarating.*

Don't just want. Choose.
                              —Patricia Benson

For many of us the fog is only beginning to clear. It takes a while to understand that all along life has been about making choices. Because we were under the influence, we inadvertently rolled into many situations with unclear intentions. Not being conscious of our choices, however, doesn't absolve us of the responsibility for making them. Now we have the opportunity, with the help of the program, to take charge of our choices. We can, with thought, make responsible choices.

We are assured the gift of empowerment when we actively take charge of our choices. We used to want things to work out without doing our part or asking for what we needed. Or we never consciously made choices. What has become so very clear is that not choosing is in fact choosing! And, no doubt, we are still saddled with the results of some of the "choices" we never intended to make. No longer does this need to be our life pattern. Today is a new day, and this program is giving us every tool we need to embark on a new course.

I will grow in confidence the more I consciously choose among my many options today.

I am learning to trust myself by getting to know
my Higher Power and then trusting the guidance
I receive.
—Helen Neujahr

Developing a relationship with our Higher Power rewards us in countless ways. The uncertainty about what to do and say in response to circumstances in our lives no longer binds us. The fear of being hurt or hurting others no longer haunts us. Uncontrollable events no longer worry us. Our lives are significantly more peaceful and positive when we get to know our Higher Power.

We felt so alone before. It's not surprising that we didn't trust ourselves. We were making decisions with no clear understanding of how they fit into the divine plan for our lives. Many of us, in fact, had no belief in a divine plan.

Hindsight, however, lets us see that our lives have been unfolding purposefully. And even though we may not have turned to a Higher Power, or not have believed in one, before getting into recovery, we were in God's care. Trusting that guidance makes our lives today so much easier.

I will be quiet so that I can hear
my Higher Power's guidance.

In the end, I define what I think, feel, and believe.
—Harriet Lerner

Many of us came into recovery confused about our beliefs. We tried to blend in with others, adopting their beliefs rather than risk looking different. Often we felt self-conscious, unsure of how to support our opinions if pressed. The game of pretend is finally over.

We don't immediately know what we think and who we are just because we get sober. But Step Four helps us start unraveling our behavior. Being alone with ourselves in this process gives us our first honest glimpse of who we are. We are dismayed by some of our qualities and heartened by others. Let's focus on the assets first.

Empowerment comes with doing a serious self-assessment. We soon understand that who we are is solely up to us. The real joy in this is realizing that who we will be, every moment of the day, is up to us too.

I am responsible for myself. What I think,
feel, believe, and say is no one's responsibility
but my own. That feels good.

A picture may be worth more than a thousand words. Yet no one can deny the impact of the simple truth.

—Jan Pishok

The truth doesn't seem so simple much of the time. Sometimes that's because we fear that if others really knew the truth about us, they wouldn't like us. Our ego can't fathom that others aren't as concerned with us as we are. Getting a healthier perspective on this can relieve us of the fear of the simple truth.

What is truth anyway? What one person defines as truth may not be consistent with another's views. Two people's perceptions of a single situation might differ dramatically but appear truthful to each one individually. There is really no such thing as the simple truth.

Knowing what is true is important, no doubt. But what may be more important is knowing that what may seem true one moment may appear otherwise the next. And that's acceptable.

I will search for the truth today. I may have to give up yesterday's truth to find it. Let me be open to it.

The more I wonder ... the more I love.
—Alice Walker

How often do we contemplate the miracles that surround us every moment of the day? Do we often stop to appreciate the evidence of these miracles? We have survived many harrowing experiences. But do we understand that our survival is one of God's miracles?

God's love for us is and has always been unconditional. No matter how bad we thought we were when we were drinking or using, God loved us. Realizing that God loves each of us equally gives us pause to wonder. Acknowledging this miracle enhances our willingness to love too.

Wonderment strengthens our humility. And from that grows love. We may have come into this recovery program believing it's impossible to love ourselves and others, but the more we cultivate our appreciation for God's intervention on behalf of us all, the easier our task.

Pausing to reflect on my good fortune today
will make loving easier.

Life isn't always that bowl full of cherries. It's sometimes very difficult and painful and we don't feel prepared for it.
—Thelma Elliott

The loss of an intimate friend, the death of a spouse, the failure to get a promotion—each can devastate us, at least for a time. It's really not possible to be emotionally prepared for many of the experiences we are destined to have. We can, however, grow accustomed to letting our Higher Power walk us through every situation. And as we grow in our acceptance of God's presence, we will discover that no experience can fully devastate us again.

The blessing that is present through painful encounters is the awareness that we are never alone. God never forces us to walk through trouble by ourselves. No opportunity to grow will ever be devoid of God's presence. God is here, now, awaiting our request for help. Asking will result in a wave of peacefulness followed by a sense of well-being that will not leave us as long as we keep our hearts open to God.

I will invite God to be with me throughout the day today. Knowing that God is present will make every experience easier to handle.

If you are truly calm, you stand a chance of surviving much, but calmness is intermittent with me.
—Florida Scott-Maxwell

The calm we feel is proportionate to the faith we have in a Higher Power. Some days are calmer than others. Why does our faith waver?

We too easily dispense with the daily routines that can help us be at peace: spending a few moments alone, reading some words of wisdom, praying to our Higher Power for care and guidance. We have probably heard someone say, "If you feel far away from God, it's not because God moved." Is it our habit to rely on God for every solution? Do we believe that every experience can benefit us as long as we acknowledge God in it? Do we make it a practice to include God in every decision we make or action we take? When we can answer yes to all of these questions, we'll discover that our faith no longer wavers. We'll know that God is close and calm is upon us.

I am calm in the company of my Higher Power. Today will run smoothly.

Pain isn't fascinating.
                    —*Sara Theism*

We often dwell with fascination on the painful situations in our lives. It's as though we're compelled to relive the experiences that traumatized us. What is this compulsion? Surely we don't court pleasure in all this pain. But that may be the insidious hook for some of us. Fortunately, this recovery program will help us, as it has helped many others, discern between healthy pleasure and unhealthy obsession.

In our youth, pain may have been so rampant in our lives that we didn't easily recognize pleasure. Now we need to follow the healthy behaviors and attitudes we observe in other women. Even though past pain may still capture our attention, we can shake our mind free of it with determination.

I will stand in awe of the miracle of my life today.
The truly fascinating thing is that
I have survived. There must be a reason.

*When you always do what you always did, you
always get what you always got. When I isolate,
I get lonely. When I reach out, someone is there.*
—Mary Timberlake

How lucky we are to have this program and the Twelve
Steps as a blueprint for living. We are building a new
foundation, one that will help us handle situations more
successfully than we did in years past. Habits are hard
to change, but we can grow in positive ways. We can
discard the old behaviors that hurt us. An inventory will
show us that we already have outgrown some of them.
We will change, given enough time and patience and
willingness. Of this we can be certain.

Oftentimes we can clearly see positive changes in our
friends. Taking note of their changes will help us see that
we are changing too. For example, we feel less self-pity or
"justifiable" anger today. We infrequently ruin an entire
day because of crippling anxiety. If we pause occasionally
and pay attention to who we are becoming, we will have
many moments worthy of celebration.

*Today I will choose not to stay stuck in the old
but to grow and change in the new.*

Whenever I am blaming someone else, I find that
I am just avoiding my own feelings of loss or grief.
—Rose Casey

The desire to blame someone else for a troubling situation is strong at times. We may even seem obsessed by our need to blame. With maturity in the program, however, we are becoming willing to take responsibility for every part of our lives. It takes lots of time, but we need to remember that this is a program of progress, not perfection.

The connection between our losses and our desire to blame others is rarely clear at first. It's not unusual for us to minimize our losses. In doing so we recognize at times a sadness or an ennui that we can't explain. Our natural response is to blame our feelings on someone else.

Fortunately, we are learning that blaming others doesn't make us feel better. The need to blame others will diminish when we learn that patience, along with practicing the principles of the program, will lift our spirits.

Today I will refrain from blaming anyone else for
circumstances in my life. Taking responsibility
may not be familiar, but I can start doing it in every
part of my life and know that I will feel good doing so.

*All my days are not wonderful, but I know what
"wonderful" is.*
—Ruthie Albert

What is "wonderful"? Is it being full of wonder? Are our
grateful moments among the wonderful ones? Perhaps.
When we're awed by the mystery of our personal salva-
tion, we experience pure wonderment. How did we get
free of our addiction and why?

Living in the aura of gratitude can make most experiences wonderful. We can't imagine why we have been
graced, but we no longer doubt that our recovery is by
design. That keeps us filled with wonder. We can choose
to focus on this feeling.

Why don't we choose to feel wonderful every day?
Maybe that's part of the disease we share. We may think
we don't deserve much happiness. It's surely possible,
however, to feel it with more regularity. There is no better
time than now to make the decision.

*My life is truly a miracle. I have been chosen
for this journey, and this fact fills me with wonder.*

*God, you're up all night. You can worry about it; I
need to get some sleep.*

—Mary S.

If only we could put our minds to rest that easily! We
can if we really want to. The Third Step makes it possible. Perhaps we assume that the Third Step doesn't work
for us because we tried it once and we still worried. We
need to try again.

Why don't we eagerly grasp this tool? Surely we don't
enjoy worrying. The truth is, we probably do. Worrying
may make us feel as if we are doing something about an
intolerable situation. The sooner we are able to believe
that worrying solves no problems, the sooner we'll be
willing to let God have a crack at them.

It takes real commitment to turn to God, over and over,
when we are consumed by worry. If we genuinely seek a
solution for our problem, we'll grow in our willingness
to try.

*I can be free of worry today. I can choose
to use the Third Step at any moment.*

It's a long trip to serenity. I better start right now.
—*Jill Clark*

Serenity often comes easiest when the search for it has ended. "Letting go and letting God" works.

What's so appealing about serenity? After all, most of us liked living on the edge before we got sober; thrill-seeking was a favorite pastime. We don't have to renounce excitement to desire serenity. But that's how it feels at first. It's possible, too, that we may not recognize serenity on its first visit. Some even mistake it for boredom. But the ease of our lives, after we grow accustomed to it, makes serenity as sought-after as excitement used to be.

Serenity allows us to appreciate more fully every aspect of our journey. Each person we encounter, every situation that calls to us, gets far more of our attention when we are calm, quiet, and focused. Only with the gift of serenity can we be all three.

Being serene is worth the effort, when we let our
Higher Power do the work of living.

*The ordinary human being thinks about twelve
thousand thoughts a day.*
—Susan Smith Jones

The mind is seldom at rest; it drifts from one scenario to another. But this busyness accomplishes little. In many instances, it sets us up for conflicts with others.

Thinking has its place in leading a responsible life. Yet making a commitment to monitor all our thoughts, and to give up willingly those that are negative toward ourselves or others, is wise.

Nothing is stopping us from thinking only beneficial thoughts. What are you feeling right now? If it's not positive, then your thoughts may be at fault. It might be helpful to review them.

*Whatever I think today is within my grasp.
Keeping my thoughts beneficial to myself
and to others will have a positive payoff.*

Situations can look very bad one day and more manageable the next. The only thing that has changed is my perspective.
—Sandra Lamberson

Attitude influences perception and outcome; it's awesomely powerful. No problem is overwhelming when we tackle it with high spirits. Everything is difficult if our moods are low.

Old-timers say AA stands for "Attitude Adjustment." Quite possibly, the longer we stay clean and sober, the more obvious it becomes that attitude is the culprit if our struggles have continued. It's fortuitous that the one aspect of our lives fully in our control is attitude.

We can have as smooth a day, on the job or at home, as we want. Our relationships can be fun and rewarding if our minds are playful and open. The people around us can handle their own circumstances adequately if we let them. What we discover about today and every day is what we seek to discover, nothing less, nothing more.

I anticipate a wonderful day today.
How it turns out is in my control.

*My life is blessed. I have riches beyond belief.
Why is it, then, that I sometimes feel lonely and
unlovable?*
—Joan Rohde

It's not easy to believe that we feel however we make
up our minds to feel. But it's true. If we are lonely, it's
because we aren't letting other people in. If we feel unlovable, it's because we aren't letting God's love in. How
we think determines how we feel. Fortunately, we have
the power to change how we think if we really want to.

How do we do that? First we need to quiet our minds
and stop the barrage of self-criticism. Then we need to
ponder the blessings in our lives, listing them, method-
ically if necessary, to acknowledge them and thus be
moved by them.

It's easy to forget that we are special. We may have to
take time each day to remind ourselves of this. Even after
years of recovery, we may forget for a spell that we are
loved and necessary and blessed in many ways.

*I won't shame myself today for thinking
negatively. Instead, I will stop, get quiet, and
think of my good fortune.*

How can I forgive others for their mistakes when
I cannot forgive myself?
—Karen Davis

Forgiveness is elusive. We aren't sure how it's done, so we close our minds to it. Resentments, on the other hand, are easy to understand. They are seductive but deadly. Why do we hang on to them? What is our payoff? Ironically, resenting someone else's behavior or their successes diminishes us. Although we get a momentary sense of superiority when we judge them, we get no long-term benefits. Much, in fact, is lost.

Forgiving others, particularly those who have harmed us, seems unfair. Why should we? Those wiser than us say "Do it." Until we have tried forgiveness we can't really know the blessing we'll receive. When we forgive others, we accelerate our growth. We see opportunities that resentment blocked. Forgiveness gives us power to open doors and step into new, inspiring circumstances.

Deliberately forgiving myself for not being perfect
will comfort me. It will allow me to go easier
on others too. We're all doing as well as we can
right now. And that's good enough.

All of us grieve differently.

—Joan Gilbertson

We have grieved over many situations. Most of us grieved over the loss of our drug of choice. Even though we were headed down a dead-end road, we still considered alcohol and other drugs to be our companions. Our choice to live meant saying good-bye to these companions and feeling lonely for a time.

We may also have to let go of friends who don't support our sobriety. We may have to leave jobs or significant relationships that hinder our growth. With every loss our emotional balance will be disrupted. The void left by the loss haunts us for a time; we respond with tears, anger, sadness, confusion, and even rage. Grief may wear a different robe with each appearance. Fortunately, we have one another to help us slip into and out of these robes of despair.

As we learn from one another's grief, we grow in our capacity to handle our own. More important, we grow in our desire to offer compassion to each hurting heart.

If I need to grieve today, I can do so freely
and fully and trust that God is close by, as are
my friends in this program. I am not alone.

God's will never takes me where his grace will not sustain me.
—Ruth Humlecker

Letting go of our own will in favor of fulfilling God's is certainly in our best interests. However, it is not always easy to do. We often cling tenaciously to a dream gone sour or a relationship long since dead because of our fear of the unknown. Although a good lesson comes from our past lives—we clearly see that God's plan would have been better for us than our own—perhaps the best lesson comes from our recovering lives today. We didn't get here all by ourselves, and God didn't help us find this program only to abandon us. We are in God's care now and always.

Believing that we will survive every experience, no matter how inadequate or frightened we feel, will come as we develop trust. Acting as if we believe that God is in charge will carry us until the belief becomes solid faith. And it will. We have been promised that. God's grace will see to it.

I will trust my life to God today.
Again and again I will turn my life over
and believe that all is well.

*As I grow older I feel so much freer to be me. This
is a real blessing that I never anticipated.*
—Marie Gubbels

Many of us didn't know who we were when we first got
into recovery. We may have mimicked other people's
actions and beliefs with no forethought, only with the
desire to fit in. One of our worst fears was that we didn't
belong. Trying to look like, act like, and think like other
women—these actions made us feel safe, inconspicuous.
That we were trapped by our fear never dawned on us.

Doing an inventory, as suggested by the program, helps
us know who we honestly are. We can see our personal
traits; we can evaluate what we want to do about qualities that cause us grief. And we can feel gratitude about
others. But, most important, we can see who we actually
are, not who we tried to be for years. The program makes
this possible. And the reward will be a peacefulness more
gratifying than any we have ever known.

No longer do we need to try someone else's behavior on
for size. What fits us, fits only us. And that is good.

*Being myself today means not watching others for
clues about what to think or say. I will listen
to my inner voice and, with her help, be true to me.*

You're right where you're supposed to be.

—*Anonymous*

Few circumstances in our lives evolve perfectly. Health problems develop, jobs don't work out, or even worse, significant others leave us. For a time we can't cope. We become angry, distraught, or full of self-pity. When a sponsor or friend says, "You're just where you need to be," we want to scream. With time, however, we usually calm down and accept this message.

A divine plan is unfolding in our lives. We don't know ahead of time the route we will take or the destination we will arrive at. Our wisdom is simply the certainty that we are "in the right place at the right time." Our Higher Power is in charge, and whatever our experiences, they are preparing us for the rest of our journey.

I am where I need to be today.
And God is planning my trip.

DECEMBER

What you praise you increase.

—Catherine Ponder

Getting trapped in negativity is far too easy. When we get stuck, we soon are overwhelmed with shame. When we're feeling miserable, we can be certain no one else is enjoying our company either.

It may feel impossible to break out of this painful cycle. Some of us may become complacent in it, yet we recognize that some women seem to experience much more peace and joy than ourselves. What do they do that's different? Careful observation reveals how accepting they are of others. They can be serene because they aren't invested in how someone else lives. This is the Serenity Prayer in action.

The easiest step in becoming like these women we admire is to begin praising what we do like in others. The more we praise their positive qualities, the less we'll focus on those parts we'd like to change. The miracle is that our inattention to the negative qualities dissipates them.

I will praise, not criticize, everyone today.
It's a decision, nothing more.
My friends will benefit, but I'll benefit even more.

First I had to learn to stand up for myself. Now I'm learning to avoid offending others while doing so. Courtesy is a virtue.
—Rose Casey

As human beings we have a tendency to let our own feelings get mixed up with the feelings of other people. Thus one of the most important discoveries we make in this program is where "we end and someone else begins."

The boundary lesson is one we probably never learned in our family of origin, and we have had many pain-filled experiences as a result. But we are learning it now. Although we occasionally step on others' toes, if we can do it with respect and grace, it is not too costly a price for learning this most elementary lesson. The key word here is *respect.* Courteously owning our behavior empowers us and sets a clear and positive example for others.

Sincere efforts to grow, if not at the expense of others, will ultimately bless us many times over. Our growth will benefit the significant people in our lives too. Sincere effort, only, is required.

I am assured that courtesy can prevail in every situation. I can be kind to other people today.

If at first you don't succeed, try again a different way.
                                        —Kay Lovatt

It's been said that Edison had more than five thousand failures on his way to inventing the electric light bulb. Why then do we need to be right the first time, every time?

Those of us in Twelve Step programs don't have a monopoly on low self-esteem, but we have our share of it. Maybe our parents or teachers were too critical, or perhaps our siblings were smarter than us in school. But each of us, no matter who we are, had—and still has—equal worth in our Higher Power's eyes.

When we know we matter in God's plan, we accept our failings as part of the learning curve. Few of us will ever meet someone who hasn't failed many times. And we admire the candor and the vulnerability of people who share their falls. Perfection isn't required. Continuing the journey is.

My definition of success determines how I feel about myself. Today I can believe that trying is succeeding.

My life is a little bit like the jazz music I play.
I stretch and explore and make some mistakes.
—Betty MacDonald

Why are we so ashamed when we make mistakes? On occasion, we may negatively judge other people for their failures, but most of the time we hardly notice them. Surely the same must be true for our failings. While we see our mistakes as glaringly evident, others give them barely a thought. We are far too absorbed in needing to be perfect.

This recovery program gives us the opportunity to change how we think and act. Maybe our family of origin heaped shame on us when we weren't perfect, but we don't have to continue this pattern.

Working on one behavior we'd like to change, one day at a time, gives us hope that we can make progress. Listening to the women we have come to admire in this program leaves little doubt that we can be successful in this pursuit. They have done it. We can too.

I am not perfect. I am willing to work on
my shortcomings today. That's enough to
satisfy my Higher Power. And me.

Every relationship is a teacher. If I don't learn the lesson, the teacher will come back.
—Brenda M. Schaeffer

We get as many chances as we need to master the lessons destined for us in this life. That's good. It removes some of the anxiety about not getting everything right the first time. While it may not be easy to admit we are relearning an old lesson, the women who share our experiences in recovery understand. And there is no shame attached, except that which we haven't yet learned to shed.

There is a positive way to meet the return of a familiar lesson. We must be willing to give it a try once again. Then we need to have faith that we're ready to make progress.

Life is relationship. We can't avoid it. We can learn to love and to accept love through relationships. We can know forgiveness through them too. Mastering these lessons is all our Higher Power hopes for us.

I am a willing student today. I will expect an important lesson from every relationship.

Some days I wonder how light can survive in a world with so much darkness. But most days I wonder how darkness can survive in a world with so much light.

—Jill Clark

Global events can be overwhelming. Nations of people are starving and at war. Earthquakes, hurricanes, and rampant poverty know no bounds. We search for hope and wonder where it is. Those walking our path are learning that it resides within. Let's be grateful.

Whether we see a situation as positive and for our good depends on our attitude. Life is as fulfilling and joyful as we decide to make it. Accepting whatever comes to us today in the spirit of gratitude will allow us to cultivate each experience for all it's worth.

Just as surely as we can cultivate a bright outlook on a day's events, we can work on a healthy perspective toward darkness. Why would we ever choose otherwise?

I don't have to relish dark thoughts today.
Remembering that God is in charge
and all is well will let me see the light.

We can't create transformational spiritual experiences by sheer will, but we can encourage them by being open to them.

—Veronica Ray

How does one define a spiritual experience? Perhaps the most we can say is that we know, oftentimes very subtly, that something wonderful has happened. We suddenly sense that we are safe, in good hands, and the pain or turmoil of our lives is passing.

Our Spiritual Guide or our Higher Power is always with us, always trying to help us, always acting as a protector and teacher. Unfortunately, many of us can't quiet our minds enough to capture the essence of God's presence in all our experiences, the mundane as well as the obviously significant. Making the Second Step of this program the foundation for daily living opens us to the myriad possibilities for the spiritual experiences we seek. "Coming to believe" is right next to "believing." Believing is next to knowing.

My life is on a spiritual plane. God's presence,
thus my safety, is as close as my next thought today.

The opinion we have of ourselves isn't just based on beliefs—it's also based on actions.
—Marie Lindquist

Seeing ourselves for who we really are is easier now that we are sober. When we work the Steps, we discover a process for living more peaceful lives. When we do an inventory, we discover who we are. Keeping track of our actions on a daily basis gives us the biggest payoff.

Trying to be our best is a challenge. Many of us are just beginning to practice taking control of our thoughts before reacting to circumstances. As a result, we have far fewer amends to make. Deciding what we want to do based on what we have consciously chosen to think is an adventure in creativity. The more we actively take charge of our own lives, the greater our rewards.

The opinion I have of myself is in my control.
I can act well today, thus think well of myself,
and vice versa.

We are ruled by that which we choose not to see.
—Clara Rosemarda

Why do we choose to ignore particular experiences? Some would say it's because we want to avoid taking the action that our conscience demands. Others suggest it's out of fear: what we can't see can't hurt us. On the contrary, unaddressed situations, whether acknowledged or not, make their demands on us. We will pay in time.

How do we make sure we are dealing with problems that affect us? Being willing to see what's going on is the first step. Focusing our thoughts on the present comes next. We need to remember the slogan "One day at a time." We certainly know that, but it's hard to live by it consistently. Little by little, we'll realize we are changing, that we are more aware of what's happening around us. The result is that we'll come to understand the influences in our lives. We'll no longer be ruled by mysteries.

What I pretend not to see has power over me.
Being consciously in charge of my life
will decrease my anxiety today.

As I learn self-acceptance, I have less need to rely on others to feel tall.
—*Kathy Kendall*

How do we develop self-acceptance? What does it feel like? During the initial stages of our recovery, self-acceptance probably didn't sound all that difficult to attain. But now we know the truth: practicing self-acceptance is rarely easy. Judging ourselves as failures and putting ourselves down for our mistakes has become habitual and "easy" to do; practicing self-acceptance, by contrast, is at first much more difficult.

While struggling to like ourselves, we perhaps fall easily into the trap of building ourselves up by judging others. As our recovery strengthens, however, we feel increasingly uncomfortable, even shameful, about judging others. And shame makes us feel even less acceptable.

Coming to believe that we have been chosen for this journey, that we have a caring Higher Power who loves us, is the best route to self-acceptance. When we're finally comfortable with the idea that we each have a gift that's unique, we'll no longer struggle to accept ourselves.

I really am as good as I need to be today.
Being here, now, means I have a unique gift to give.

The Twelve Steps have taught me to feel my
pain—and then walk through it.

—Joan Rohde

Getting clean and sober has not meant an end to the pain in our lives. Being human gives us many opportunities to feel and grow through painful experiences. But what is different now is that we have the support of a loving God and the Twelve Steps to give us hope and clarity. We also have the friendship of many women who understand us. Our journey through the unknown is made in the company of these friends.

Sometimes we wonder why we have been graced. Most of us are befriending women who still struggle without the benefit of this program. We see our former selves in them, and we wish we could give them what we now have. In our past, every experience had the potential to devastate us; today no experience is too much for us to handle.

We are free: free to enjoy every moment; free of the fear that we have to solve our problems alone; free of dread about what the future may hold.

I am looking forward to my experiences today,
for they will be the right ones for my growth.
God will help me handle the hard parts.

When you are down, get back up and fight!
                                                    —*Iris Timberlake*

Our attitude determines how we handle every experience. If we feel defeated by circumstances—say we've lost a job or a friend has abandoned us—we will not be ready for the next opportunity our Higher Power has in store for us. No door is ever closed without another one being opened. However, if we are focused on what's no longer ours, we'll miss what can be.

This is not to say we shouldn't grieve our losses. In order to accept them, we must feel them. Then we need to get back on our feet and go on with this moment, this day, this life. Not to do so is to deny trust in one's Higher Power. The Third Step promises that we have a caring God in charge. Yesterday's closed doors didn't mean our lives were over. Nor will today's.

I will relish the strength I feel today
when I remember that God is opening (and closing)
all the right doors for me.

When I started feeling the pain of my story, my healing process began.
—Helen Neujahr

Healing is a crucial element in our recovery, and the Fourth and Fifth Steps are oftentimes the catalyst to get the process going. Doing a careful Fourth Step inventory helps us to recognize the sources of our wounds. Sharing our darkest secrets in a Fifth Step takes away some of the shame that has kept us sick.

Forgiving ourselves for our past transgressions is a hurdle we must clear in order to sustain the healing process. The bonds of intimacy we are forging with other women help us know how very alike we are. None of us are without a tarnished past. Sharing our stories will help us heal.

Forgiving the other significant people in our lives is also necessary for real healing to occur. The past abuse we may have suffered left scars. But we can heal. We can help each other heal too. The Steps and our Higher Power will guide us.

Sharing some of my story with another person today will help both of us heal. God will help me find the words.

To let go is to wander often into dark, unknown, scary places. The darkness fades as we stretch out our hand and feel the touch, the grasp, of another.
—Margo Casey

It's not surprising that we fear letting go. We spent years trying to control other people and circumstances. And just because we generally failed at our attempts doesn't mean that we understood why. Most of us have continued to think, "Maybe this time . . ." How lucky we are to have this program as a daily guide. We are getting the message. Some of us may take longer hearing it, but all of us will learn that letting go is possible. Every time we do so successfully, we ensure that we will let go even more quickly the next time.

Besides the serenity that comes when we let go, we feel the soft touch of our Higher Power, who has been awaiting our reach for help. Letting go gives us not only peace but also the spiritual connection that will help us let go more quickly the next time.

I can let go of any problem that troubles me today. God will be there to take my burden and my hand.

*It takes two to tango, and my husband and I
tangoed for nearly sixty-three years.*
—Thelma Elliott

Spending time with another human being means having plentiful opportunities for compromise and artful negotiation. It also means putting another's needs and wants before our own on occasion. To fruitfully share even portions of our lives, we must be willing to be available to each other.

We weren't created to be sole survivors, independent of other people. We have been introduced to many individuals because of the path we are meant to travel together. Our significant other is one of those from our community of travelers. With that person, we have the opportunity to learn new truths and to grow in wisdom about the art of vulnerability and compromise. No doubt, the most profound of our lessons is learning to let go.

The gift of learning how to let go is that we can apply it everywhere once we've come to understand its power in our lives. And our dance with others will never be the same.

*I will be willing to back away from a tense
encounter today. I don't need my way to be okay.*

It is how much love we put in the doing that makes our offering something beautiful.
—Mother Teresa

Mother Teresa's words aren't new to most of us. Program sponsors often suggest this idea to us too. What we give comes back to us.

We often note people who excel on the job, in a sport, at a creative pursuit. We may envy them and think we should excel at everything we try. "Why are we so lacking in talent?" we wonder.

We have not been shortchanged. The truth is, we may not have learned to concentrate our attention so fully on an activity that we come to love the experience simply for the sake of the experience. Those who excel are not easily distracted by others' actions or their own ongoing inner dialogues or fear of failure. Their intense focus and love for what they are doing allows their talent to be realized.

When we're putting love into our actions, we, too, will discover our own excellence.

It's not what I do but how I do it that counts.
Being in love with my life today is a choice I can make.

When I remember to listen and savor another's experience as valuable and sacred, I touch a sense of mystery.
—Rita Casey

As much as we may want to deny it, few of us are truly attentive listeners. We try to listen. We even work hard to keep our own obsessive thoughts quiet. But turning our entire attention to a friend in need is a trait we may never perfect. Even so, listening is a worthy pursuit, because very frequently God's wisdom comes to us through another person's words.

Our intimate moments with another soul are never accidental or inconsequential. We are like dancers in a ballet. Each of our movements has its complement in another's movement. We have been drawn together to complete the story for one another. And it's imperative to hear another's words if we are to fulfill our very special role. We can know God's will if we listen closely to the words of others.

We should remember that God is present always in our friends with the message our souls await.

Dear God, help me listen today to your message and it is expressed through my friends.

The events in our lives happen in a sequence in time, but in their significance to ourselves they find their own order.
—Eudora Welty

Recalling the distant past, or even last week, helps us realize how little we remember of the very events that compose our lives. We may vividly remember the slights we felt from others, the defeats, and the embarrassments, but the millions of ordinary details have vanished. Have they not a place in our histories too?

Getting a more balanced perspective on who we have been and who we are becoming is one of the rewards of this program. As we discover who we are in greater detail, we become more aware of the quiet moments in our lives. Events that seemed of little significance before can now enlighten us. Our personal and family histories have a part in who we struggle to become. Let's honor all of them.

What may seem significant to me today
may be less important in the years ahead.
I'll not pass judgment, but honor
all of it as uniquely my own.

No iron bars can hold a bad relationship together.
If it is good, a gossamer thread suffices.
—Jan Pishok

We aren't fooled into believing a bad relationship is good. However, we may stay far too long, unwilling to leave it. Why is it so hard to close some doors?

We may have been taught to deny our pain. When we acknowledge the hurt or anger that results from any relationship, action becomes necessary. Making a change, perhaps deciding to leave, is never easy. But what a shame it is to stay in a relationship that no longer nurtures us. Why do we do it? For many, it's the fear of the unknown. We have learned to tolerate the pain. We have this program, and using it—particularly our sponsors and the Steps—will give us the courage to do what we need to do for ourselves. But we must make the first move.

If I am not happy in a relationship today,
I will use the tools of the program
to sort out my options.

I had always thought self-esteem was a state of being. Now I realize it's the constant decision to love myself regardless of circumstances, all day long.

—Mary Casey

What does it mean to love ourselves all day long? It means loving ourselves even when we feel shame for having yelled at a friend. It means loving ourselves even when we secretly wish harm on another. It means continuing to love ourselves even when we let opportunities to do something good for other people slip by.

There will be days when we need to make the conscious decision to love ourselves moment by moment. We will never be perfect, but we can be better people than we were in the past. We are making progress. A brief personal inventory will reflect this: perhaps we are learning to think before we act; perhaps we are treating friends or even strangers less critically; perhaps we are seeing the benefits of loving others unconditionally.

In time we will realize the gains we have made. We will see that it is possible to love ourselves fully, even though we have not become perfect.

I will love my every attempt to be kind and thoughtful today. I will forgive each of my failures.

We get love, assistance, and companionship in our relationships; we must each find our purpose and our strength in our own soul.
—Jane Nakken

Relationships offer us not only opportunities to express love but also experiences that develop a full range of emotions. We learn about anger and forgiveness. We experience joy and self-pity. We cultivate trust and learn to live with occasional fear. Without relationships we'd live colorless, shallow lives.

Relationships reveal our character, our values. People come to know us by how we react to friends and strangers, by our willingness to let others travel their own path, by our decision to be guided by our inner voice rather than the prodding of others. Others' responses also help us know who we are. We may learn more about ourselves from how others respond to us than from any other source.

I will notice how others respond to me today.
I'll discover who they think I am by how they treat me.

*Would you rather be cursing the darkness or
lighting the candles?*
—Connie Hilliard

Feeling despair over situations, be they grave or less
significant, can become habitual. Prior to recovery, our
first response to virtually every circumstance that didn't
please us may have been despair. How grateful we can
be that we are finally learning to see the glass as half
full rather than as half empty. It's really not that difficult
to do, and the small shift in our perspective results in
a huge attitude adjustment. This in turn influences the
outcomes we experience.

How powerful is our attitude! No longer can we be
overwhelmed by even the most dire of circumstances if
we remember to stay in charge of our attitude. Taking
active charge of our responses to the events in our lives
also strengthens our character and helps us to develop the
integrity we long for. Our assets will flourish with seem-
ingly little effort if we let every situation be an opportunity to demonstrate a positive attitude. Adherence to this
decision promises profound pleasures!

*I can make my day as bright as I choose.
My attitude can light my way.*

It is a spiritual act to use your own eyes and ears
and mind and heart to know the world in your
way of knowing, to live in the world in your way
of living.
—Patricia Benson

The codependency we struggled with most of our lives
kept us from using our own eyes and minds and hearts
to see the world. Because we felt it was our job to take
care of others' feelings, we missed the opportunities to
know and respect our own feelings and perspectives on
the world.

Recovery is making it possible for us to know and live
in our world, and what a gift that is! The Steps guide us
to a clearer understanding of who we are, sponsors help
us appraise our plans and actions, and our Higher Power
offers us the strength, courage, and belief to do what we
need to do.

We may always need reminders that seeing the world
from where we stand is appropriate, healthy, and spiritual. Letting others have their own perspective is likewise
appropriate. This program is designed to help us do both.

I will not let others take charge of how I see
the events of my life today. I will rely on God
to help me be true to my own vision.

God's gifts are slowly revealed.

—*Michele Fedderly*

We are so certain about what we need and when we need it that we become anxious and agitated. Patience is a virtue, we know, but we're not moved to practice it when an outcome in our lives is at stake.

How fortunate that we have the gift of hindsight. The impatience we feel now is not unlike what we've felt thousands of times, yet God has never let us down. We may not have gotten exactly what matched our will, but we see now that God had many gifts in store for us. In every case they were right for us, even though we may have resisted them at first.

When we are in pain we think God has forgotten us. On the contrary, our pain is often caused by not acknowledging the direction God is trying to give us. At the right time, in the right place, the right gift or direction will always be offered. Let's remember that and be grateful.

God's gifts are revealed when the time is right.
Today I do not travel this path alone.

I don't have to believe in the same things that my loved ones believe in, in order to love them.

—*Karen Davis*

One of the most valuable gifts we can receive from this program is learning how to let go of other people. Giving up our struggle to control how friends and family members think and behave and feel will bless us with an exhilarating freedom.

Most of us never realized we could let others live their own lives. We sincerely thought we needed to help others see life as we saw it. Certainty that we were right in all matters was part of our disease. Letting others be themselves meant we weren't in control.

We've come to understand that, in fact, we aren't in control and never were. But now we are glad for that understanding. Now we are free to spend our time on creative pursuits that please us rather than spinning our wheels trying to make people follow us. We each have a path to follow, and we are growing in our gratitude for that realization.

I may want my loved ones to think like me,
but I will let them make their own choices today.
Really loving them means really letting them go.

We need to let the old go, so the new can emerge.
—*Peggy Bassett*

When we first entered the program, we heard the saying "One door must close before another can open." That baffled us, even while it gave us comfort. It helped that women we looked up to found solace in the slogan. Their experiences, shared in the meetings, taught us understanding. Each time we fought against a changing condition, someone we admired was able to remind us of its value.

Now we are the truth-bearers for the newcomers. Over time we have come to believe that every experience has special meaning. When something new begins to tap us on the shoulder, that's our cue to let something else go. Newcomers need our demonstration of how it works. No doubt, before this day or this week has passed, we'll each have an opportunity to close one door and open another. Let's make sure we share what we learn with someone else.

I am someone's teacher today. I will not
fight circumstances that are changing
but accept that their passing is my opportunity.

A crisis is only a turning point.

—Anne Lindthorst

The sting is removed from a crisis when we accept it as a turning point. Our lives have been full of turning points. A moment's reflection brings to mind crises that moved us to far better places. For instance, we may not have counted on finding sobriety and this program of recovery, but a significant crisis delivered us here.

Because we remember how frightening a crisis can be, let's make an effort to help our sisters gain a healthier perspective on the turning points in their lives. When we're in a rocking boat, it's not easy to remember that a storm ushers in clear skies. Sharing this information with our struggling sisters keeps us from forgetting it too.

With enough faith, we can look forward to the lessons and growth experiences life offers. We'll never doubt their contribution to our developing nature.

I need not fear a troubling situation today.
It is offering me a lesson I am ready to learn.

The work of adult life is not easy.
—Gail Sheehy

What does being an adult mean to most of us? Perhaps taking full responsibility for all of our actions comes quickest to mind. While using alcohol and other drugs, we were prone to blame our troubles on the nearest warm body. And to our detriment, we often got away with it.

We may still tend to blame others for the strife in our lives. We aren't immediately willing to go from our assumed blamelessness to full responsibility, just because we gave up our drug of choice. But the people who share our lives now are helping us accept the responsibility that has been ours all along.

The principles of AA make recovery more palatable. We know we are ready for the changes that are promised, or we wouldn't be here now.

*I will do my work today. I will accept
responsibility for all my actions,
and I will think before opening my mouth.*

In childhood I was told that if I have faith, health,
and love, I have everything. As an adult I know
it's true.
—Mardy Kopischke

Over the years we may have wasted lots of energy seeking material possessions, certain that one more outfit, a
new hairstyle, or a better-paying job would fix our problems. Nurturing our health, practicing the presence of a
Higher Power, or giving love were low on our "to do" list.
Other people may have even suggested these practices
to us, but we didn't understand the payoff.

Now in recovery we are beginning to reap the benefits of such practices. We have discovered that the principles of the program, when lived fully, cultivate our faith,
strengthen our health, and teach us the meaning of being
loved. These in turn make giving love to others easier.
In the process we realize that everything we ever erro-
neously hoped to gain through possessions can be ours
when we follow the simple suggestions of this program.

I am wiser now that I know
how to nurture faith, health, and love.

*No matter what happens, I must get on with
my life.*
—Ruth Humlecker

Life is full of uncertainties: people we love come and go,
opportunities knock and then disappear, jobs sour, and
goals become unachievable. We are forever adjusting
to the unexpected. However, remembering that there
is one constant in our lives, a Higher Power who will
support and guide us, helps us accept whatever comes
our way.

There is no conspiracy against us. It may feel that way
when we are overwhelmed by or unprepared for a crisis.
But there is a plan for us. And it fits only us. The most
productive lesson we can learn is to trust that this is so.
We can learn to appreciate every experience for the part
it plays in our lives.

Our lives continue to unfold. Each day brings us closer
to the woman we are destined to be. Let's get on with it!

*No matter what happens,
I am in good hands. My course has been set.
I'll look for the good in all of today.*

Every ending is part of a beginning. Every loss is part of an emptiness that can be filled with newness.
—Jan Lloyd

The door that is closing today may fill us with dread; however, we can find relief when we recall other endings that unexpectedly led to new friendships, better jobs, wonderful opportunities.

Life is a process. Every event in our lives is connected to what has gone before and what will come after. There are no real endings; there are only new opportunities for growth and change. For most of us it's a matter of changing our perspective. The difference is subtle yet extremely powerful, and our lives will never feel the same.

I look forward to these twenty-four hours!
I can be glad for everything that comes
to me, trusting in its blessing.

Acknowledgments

When I decided to do another meditation book for women in recovery, I felt compelled to include, in some way, the many women who had written me after they had read *Each Day a New Beginning*. I know I have many friends all over the world, and just knowing we walk the same spiritual path helps my sobriety on a daily basis. It also keeps me conscious of the mystery of God's role in our lives. I unquestionably never expected to be where I am, doing what I'm doing. Had I fulfilled *my* plans, I'd clearly be dead. That God had planned something better for me overwhelms me with gratitude. Each day, in fact, God generally has something better for me than my limited mind can imagine.

When I started *Each Day a New Beginning*, I never expected other books would follow. All of my books have since been inspired in some measure by the wonderful women in my life, women I met in AA, Al-Anon, and elsewhere. Because I wanted them to share more in the process of this book, I requested a line or two of their own wisdom to trigger the meditations contained herein. As a result, this book comes from all of us to *all of you*.

Because these women are so special, I want to publicly thank them. Loving thanks to Cathy Stone, Sandy Lamberson, Ruth Casey, Anne Marie Nelson, Dawn Gessner, Gail Nelson, Connie Hilliard, Robbie Rocheford,

Kathy McGraw, Lisa Keyes, Ruth Humlecker, Elizabeth
Farrell, Karen Davis, Marianne Lunde, Carlotta Posz,
Marie Gubbels, Helen Casey, Helen Neujahr, Phyllis
Elliott, Sharon Walters, Rita Casey, Julie Riebe, Richie
Berlin, Patricia Benson, Kelley Vickstrom, Mary
Larson, Laurel Lewis, Iris Timberlake, Eileen Fehlen,
Molly McDonald, Joan Rohde, Margo Casey, Mardy
Kopischke, Thelma Elliott, Joan Gilbertson, Rose Casey,
Chris DeMetsenaere, Anne Arthur, Mary Casey, Robyn
Halsema, Jan Lloyd, JoAnn Reed, Michele Fedderly,
Mary Timberlake, Sarah Desmond, Abby Warman, Julie
B., Jill Clark, Georgette Vickstrom, Jan Pishok, Dudley
Martineau, Betty MacDonald, Jane Nakken, Mary Zink,
Mary Norton Gordon, Kathy Kendall, Joy Sommers, Kay
Lovatt, Ruthie Albert, Louise Rice, and Kathleen Tierney
Andrus. The many other women I have quoted come
from all walks of life. Their wisdom spoke to me through
articles or books. I wanted to share it with you.

My acknowledgments wouldn't be complete without
thanking the wonderful people at Hazelden who have
supported my efforts these many years, particularly
Linda Peterson, Mark Crea, Sharon Walters, Pat Benson,
Shirley Jones, Peter Butler, Rebecca Post, Judy Delaney,
and Jeff Petersen. To Harry Swift I owe a powerful debt of
gratitude for his belief in my first effort, *Each Day a New
Beginning*. Without his support, the rest could not have
happened. I also want to thank my husband Joe, who has
been present through every book and who makes every
part of my life feel like the special hand of God is involved.

About the Author

Karen Casey, PhD, is the author of twenty-nine books. Her first, *Each Day A New Beginning: Daily Meditations for Women*, published in 1982, has sold millions of copies. She has been committed to helping people walk the path of spiritual recovery since she first stepped into a Twelve Step room in 1974. Her recent books have focused more specifically on healing our relationships, which is necessary if we want to be at peace. Her most recent book, *20 Things I Know for Sure: Principles for Cultivating a Peaceful Life*, quite specifically focuses on being at peace in all of our encounters.

About Hazelden Publishing

As part of the Hazelden Betty Ford Foundation, Hazelden Publishing offers both cutting-edge educational resources and inspirational books. Our print and digital works help guide individuals in treatment and recovery, and their loved ones.

Professionals who work to prevent and treat addiction also turn to Hazelden publishing for evidence-based curricula; digital content solutions; and videos for use in schools, treatment and correctional programs, and community settings. We also offer training for implementation of our curricula.

Through published and digital works, Hazelden Publishing extends the reach of healing and hope to individuals, families, and communities affected by addiction and related issues.

For more information about Hazelden publications,
please call **800-328-9000**
or visit us online at **hazelden.org/bookstore**.

Other Titles That May Interest You

The Promise of a New Day
A Book of Daily Meditations
BY KAREN CASEY AND MARTHA VANCEBURG

Happy or sad, challenging or routine, each day makes demands on us. These daily readings offer wisdom and inspiration to help us make the most of each day.

Item 1045

Worthy of Love
Meditations on Loving Ourselves and Others
BY KAREN CASEY

For those who struggle to love and be loved. *Worthy of Love* offers fifty-two wisdom-filled meditations. Favorite Hazelden author Karen Casey clarifies the varieties of love: the love we show friends, family, a lover, even ourselves.

Item 5005